Redwood Writers
2018 Poetry Anthology

Phoenix

Out of Silence ... and then

Les Bernstein and Fran Claggett-Holland
Co-editors

Susan Gunter and Judy Anderson
Editorial Assistants

Linda L. Reid
Board Liaison

An anthology of poetry
by Redwood Writers
A branch of the
California Writers Club

Redwood Writers 2018 Poetry Anthology:
Phoenix
Out of Silence … and then

Editors
Les Bernstein and Fran Claggett-Holland

© 2018 by Redwood Writers
All rights reserved

ISBN: 978-0997754445

Book design
by Jo-Anne Rosen
Wordrunner Publishing Services

Cover art
by Warren Bellows

Published by Redwood Writers Press
PO Box 4687
Santa Rosa, California 95402

Just Flung Out from Sleep

We know each other through our poems.
How amazing that we know so many people.
Some we know only one way; we know them
but they have never seen our words,
flung out from sleep or crafted carefully
as we reach out to the world.
But when we read your poems
the words perfect on the page,
saying things we almost thought
but never had the words for,
then we know each other well and true.

— Fran Claggett-Holland

Contents

Redwood Writer Award of Merit Poets

Out of Silence

Poems from Sonoma County Poet Laureates

... and then

Introduction

As children, many of us read the myth of the phoenix, the colorful fire-colored bird that rose, newborn, from the ashes of her nest. The phoenix myth occurs all over the world each with many variations, but all with one common theme—rising from the fire of the nest to a new life. Here in Sonoma County, the phoenix soon became a story that people discussed over and over when they came together after the fires to rebuild or redesign their lives.

As we considered the way poetry serves both to express what we know and to find new ways to say things, thus opening up new ways to conceive of our lives, it seemed right to rename the anthology we were building with poetry. We have retained the original name—"Out of Silence … and then" but subsumed it into the larger theme of the mythic bird, the Phoenix.

In this collection of poems, you will find the heart of Sonoma County: you will read poems that depict everyday life; you will find poems that express our feelings about families, about the natural world; you will see evidence of the imagination let loose; you will experience the heartbreak of loss, both personal and shared. And you will read poems that demonstrate the enduring belief in the basic power of the human spirit.

We have many to thank: First of all, we thank all those members of Redwood Writers who contributed their poems to this volume. It takes courage to submit one's work to the public eye, especially for first-time submitters. We thank our editorial assistants, Susan Gunter and Judy Anderson, who not only read widely, but offered suggestions for improvement; one of the foremost purposes of Redwood Writers is to encourage the improvement of our craft, and we take this goal seriously.

We are extremely happy to acknowledge Warren Bellows, an artist and poet who is well-known in Sonoma County and beyond. Warren once again donated one of his inspiring paintings, which he had named "Hope," as the cover of Phoenix, an anthology which encompasses both the beauty of Sonoma County and the spirit of the people who live here. Whether directly affected or indirectly, we all felt the losses of so many. And all of us were touched by the story of that courageous dog Odin, who saved his goats while the fire destroyed the house and farm buildings around him.

The first poems in this book are by the three Redwood Writers Award of Merit poets, writers whose poems exhibited an unusual degree of quality; they are Barbara Armstrong, Betty Les, and Mark Meierding.

In our desire to feature Sonoma County writers who demonstrate excellence and commitment both to their craft and to our community, we invited our previous poet laureates to send us poems. We are proud to have poems by Terry Ehret, Geri Digiorno, Gwynn O'Gara, Bill Vartnaw, Katherine Hastings, and Iris Jamahl Dunkle. We also acknowledge those laureates who are no longer with us, but whose work inspired so many in our community: Don Emblen, David Bromige, and Mike Tuggle.

We reached out to other local poets of acknowledged excellence; here you will find powerful poems by Ed Coletti, Jonah Raskin, and Larry Robinson. We also invited Clare Morris, after her reading at the community event "Rising from the Ashes," and Rebecca del Rio after reading her work on Larry Robinson's online poetry site. We thank them for sharing their poems with us.

We extend our thanks to Redwood Writer volunteer proofreaders: Skye Blaine, Harry Reid, Belinda Riehl, and Angel Stork. Our book design genius Jo-Anne Rosen, our meticulous webmaster Joelle Burnette; and our go-to-for-all questions Linda Loveland Reid have made this book possible. Our thanks to them and to the Redwood Writers Board of Directors for supporting this project.

the editors,
Fran Claggett-Holland
and
Les Bernstein

Redwood Writer
Award of Merit Poets

Barbara Armstrong

Betty Les

Mark Meierding

Barbara Armstrong

Pursuing Dylan Thomas

For the True Prince of Wales 1914-1953
with gratitude for the gift of your words.

Tousled Blue-eyed Son of Wales,
What did you call yourself:
The Common Thread,
The Bright Pretender,
The Ridiculous Sea Dandy?

O' you were easy then
In the greening of your days,
"Drunk with a drug that's
Smoking in a girl," you said,
But wary of the thistle in her kiss,
The muscling in of love.

I dogged your threadbare track
Up Horseback Hill by fox light
Stood by until your handmade moon
Broke brilliant across the steepled vale,
And your second cigarette
Was silenced on a stone.

Along the margins
Of your huffing sea I followed.
Past rowdy wind-burned bluffs
To docks heaped high with fishing nets.
I sought your reeling stanzas
On the salt stung air.

Cormorants stood sentinel
On every post, wings
Outstretched like weather vanes.
Was that your skiff,
Untethered and adrift
In deeper water?

Shape Shifter

Not some legendary bird
with wings of flame
nor cartoon dragon blowing
lazy rings of smoke
across a movie screen
but animate living force
charting its own course,
asserting its own reign.

Fire beyond our imagining
born in an arc of wanton power,
spurred on by stiff diablo winds
devours the residues of summer
stokes on the scaffolds
of our droughted woodlands.
Climbing towers of its own making,
it vaults our man-made boundaries
laying waste, incurring chaos
wherever it touches down.

Citizens, awake!
The flames are mirrored now
in your bedroom windows!
Even the distant
mountains are on fire.
Rouse your children
still dressed in the soft clothes
of their dreaming.
Sirens are screaming
Run for your lives!

Avenues have lost their names.
Guttural groans as home after
home submits its bones
to leaden plots of soot and cinder.
Ladders and hubcaps liquefy
to counterfeited silver ingots.

Ghostly moths of paper ash
drift for miles like scripts of
people's lives suspended and
displaced in other people's yards.
A tetherball explodes;
its chain still whips the pole
knelling the death of yet
another neighborhood.

Red-eyed water wagons
crowd the freeways.
Determined troops
five thousand strong,
strap on their helmets,
arm themselves with
mattocks, shovels, canvas
hoses heavy in their arms.
So small they seem in silhouette
against the pre-dawn conflagration.
The water cannons blast,
dozers shoulder back the earth,
copters dip the lakes and
reservoirs like dragonflies,
bombers let their blood-red
banners of retardant fly.
Co-ordinates and strategies
are on our side,
that and the mercy of
complicit rain.

Seventeen days and nights, and then…
the fire, contained and starved,
abandons its amorphous rage,
huffing its acrid breath
retreats into the nimbus.
And if ancient Chinese lore is true,
it will become again a silk cocoon
large enough to house a universe.

Barbara Armstrong

One Small Devoted Hand

In the remote mountains of Tibet,
an ancient monastery warehouses
thousands of thangkas, tightly scrolled,
preserved in tin boxes, a testament
to the perpetuation of faith beyond centuries.

Kneeling on stone
  a young monk in a saffron robe
  leans toward his canvas of woven silk;
  pigments of cobalt and vermillion
  wet the slender brushes,
  bristles fine as lashes.

He'll replicate the luminous halo
  of a certain Buddha in a
  garden of measured flowers.
  proportions are exact,
  and in the end
  he does not

sign the piece.

Old Friends

It's all in the noticing
what's there or not
what we perceive
what we are open to perceiving

The human eye is a tricky organ
so influenced by the brain
and then there is the heart
which swings open and shut

It took me five years
looking at the rock formation
five years of being drawn to it
touching it, studying it up close

Before I saw the smooth gray
drape of skin
elephantine body and legs
the well-placed eyes

Two old friends
one slightly turned toward the other
sharing a private thought

Where is Pablo Picasso

who else could capture
the horrors of war in a
single painting

the surprise of attack
raw terror and confusion
anguish and death
piercing in their abstraction
Guernica stares back at us
huge and still on the museum wall

so large you are forced
to back away
take it in slowly
your eyes sweeping
the painting
like bombers swept the village

who will capture the atrocities
of our time
which image among thousands
will we point to
saying this is what happened
this must be stopped

Salt

we are born
with the taste of it
on our lips

salt, from that
inland sea

is it any wonder
we spend our lives
seeking the ocean
to feel again

the salt spray on our face
weightless
floating and rolling
the sense of belonging
imprinted on our limbs

.

Seduction

Every child knows the snakes
are hidden everywhere—
in broom closets and attic trunks and
Mother's locked jewel case.
Menace is the natural state of closed things.

Like whispers down dark hallways,
snakes wait within, and bravery
is only a fabley word.
Open the lid, and if none wriggles out,
you were lucky—this time.
No danger was ever disproved by a missing snake.

Yet secret places tease
like the tingle of honey on your tongue,
so five tiny fingers will creep
toward latch or clasp or key
as if it had just come out of the kiln.
Snakes love heat,
and snakes love little fingers,
and snakes can spy the narrow wishes
inside young eyes. Oh, yes,
the snakes are too, too wise.

The Long Beach

Brown skins, white skins, scurrying,
umbrellas, strollers, retrievers on joggers' leashes—
these vertical sensations
against a vibration of horizon. Bellowing surf
dwarfs the speech of humans,
condensing their dialogues
into gesture and screech.
The rest of conversation recedes
into ocean's hem of froth.

Language recedes, yes, but not the hourglass
curve of the tide, which is gradually growing
into the crescent of this shore.
Sand that was just dry
and individual as curlews' beaks
will sink into the collective identity of slush.
Soon we must remove our canvas chairs,
our faded towels and plastic buckets,
our cameras that try to arrest
the sentient profiles of vanishing familiars.

Still
the waves' tumbling blast
calms us.
We've heard this sound in wombs, or before—
the insistent thrum of ocean's load
upon a terrace of land,
investing its voice
into the bellies of generations.

Silenced by waves' roar,
so much that could be said
reverberates within the conch
of each mind's thoughts,
where white water encircles bare ankles
like invited snakes,
drawing us in and drawing us,
dreaming, out.

Mark Meierding

Tree of Books

Each
December
In   Oaxaca's
Museo de   Artesanías
two hundred   books
dangle   near each other   from the ceiling,
each   at its own   height
from its   own wire,
making   the shape of   a   Christmas tree.
Collections   of cuentos,   historias,   poesía,
spreading   cone-shaped   as the Virgin's vestments.
If anyone   should push or pull   one wire,
they   would   tangle
tight as twists   of winter doubt.   But no one   does.
Bright   as Advent birds   with bows,   this flock   floats tiny
at the top   and full   around the hem,   yet no volume
touches the floor.   Room for presents   in that nave of space   below.
Or perhaps   we   are that tree,   and the books
are our gift.

Out of Silence

Speak Beauty Silence

Beauty blind.
Hold me still and raise me up to your
Expectations.
Since when do men have the privilege of deciding your worth?
Since always.
Since their muscles dominate and their psyche is challenged by the
Strength of
Woman.

Men, those who have mastered the art of holding us up while
Pinning us down to the salty earth.

Do they not know we are made of earth?
That we get our breath from nature?

Can they not see our strength is found in the wind and dirt,
the water and fire,
that shape the world?

Time will hold us up when our forms cannot.
Our Earth Mother feeds us in secret circles,
Provides food with quiet glances and subtle smiles in children's
    playgrounds.
Both in plain sight and invisible to
Mankind.

Holding tight to the hands of our sisters, we know the truth.
Do not let go.
We will define your secret beauty.
We will choose.
Powerful and pure, our connection is our
Victory.

Backdraft

you bear down on me, all heat and sweat
each acrid breath more shallow than the last
I am tinder

I imagine hooves of fleeing deer
ash laden birds falling
And I swear I can hear the trees cracking

shovels against flame, your body against mine
soft flesh engulfed
what rises from this smoke?

fire—our backdrop, our foreground, our foreclosure
the last patch of sky surrendering to gray
even the sun yields to this burn

I am the fleeing deer, the falling birds
my wings beat against your futility
no suppression, no containment

I am lost in your backdraft

Judy Anderson

Miguel's Garden

Kiwi fruit hangs from the aging arbor,
branches brittle and leafless. Orange trees—
fragrant bounty once shared by all—now
the roosting place for a murder of crows,
the fallen fruit, aphrodisiac for insects.
Merlot and pinot grapes ferment on the ground.
Drunken robins, gorged on sugar slam my windows,
leave ghostly outlines and downy feathers. Stunned,
they tremble in the weeds where the cat waits.
Tomatoes, over ripe and split, spill their seeds, next year's
bounty lost. Blackbirds spear hornworms, feast on spiders.
By night, rodents vie for the spoils.

Miguel sits at the window and waits, his body too
host to unbidden scavengers.

Architecture

The kitchen holds the heart and soul of home.
So says the architect, who builds, then leaves.
And of this home, I think it could be true,
but whose heart, is a question I would pose.
The woman at the stove whose bitter tears
dilute her soup and every fleeting dream?
The man whose footfall prompts a taste of fear?
The children seated at the table, mute?
A home can house a broken heart and soul.
No joyful recollections echo here.

The Wonder and the Why

Who knows why the queen termite flies?
The spectacle of grace-lace wings
helicoptering across the dusk end
of September Sonoma skies.
Her search for a hidden place
to birth a wood-hungry army
to gnaw buildings to their bare footings.
A twining of destruction and wonder.

And who knows why the harvest moon
casts purple pools of light under coastal oaks
that glow against the midnight hillside?
Why the sight of it startles the insomniac
padding past the picture window
into breath-taking awakening?
An astonishment of splendor.

Or why the inky tabby cat stalks the innocence
of burrowing owls and nesting squirrels
as the season leans
toward bone chill and drizzle
and sunrise and sunset clock closer
to shorter, hungrier days?

Why? Because nothing is without
its intricate design, its supreme scheme
which is working, even now,
through the purpled hillside,
through the pajamaed man at the window.
Through the piercing curl of tabby's claws,
the grace-lace wings shed at the threshold

by the fertile queen, the changeable tilt
of Earth's circuit around the sun.

Elegance seeps over and under time
into seasoned richness.
A progress that unfolds to its own cadence
one termite bite by one curling cat's claw.
To nail the detail is to miss the moment.
Heisenberg's certainty of uncertainty assures us
place and pace can each be known
precisely
but never both at once.

Everything swirls within its given constellation.
Sudden revelations are only timeless
bits of elegance pooling, gnawing
under moonlit cover all along.

Barbara Beatie

To my Mother who loved Amy Lowell

Today, "The Garden by Moonlight," found me. I wish that we had shared this poem. I wish we had read this poem together, you and me.

If I had known that time was fleeting, we could have taken our wine out to your grandmother's garden, to the corner with the orange lilies that knew her, and read this poem in the twilight by candlelight. I would have watched your face betray your sheer delight with words; a joy that you've let slip away as friends steal your time, and writing gets put into a hallway closet with the winter blankets.

I would have seen you, if we had had enough wine, you would have let your guard down, and you would have read the poem in your voice trained by Mr. Guyman's drama classes. I would have been a child again, all at once enchanted, and yet afraid of your huge talent, talent underemployed now at church fundraising events or the thank-you speeches at the PTA. There was so much more!

To watch you accept this diminished life you created scarred me like a burn that periodically broke open but refused to heal. Why didn't I know then how to summon your gifts and give you the light to breathe and grow? How could I have expected you to know how to do that for me?

If we had read this Amy Lowell poem together, in the garden, I would like to imagine I would have caught you in that rarest moment with time to yourself, your courage high, your confidence returned. I wish the poem, now newly discovered, and valued, and loved, had compelled you to tell your story through your writing, your moon shimmer talent finally unfettered and in the starlight, like the firefly, in motion, free, incandescent.

I wish that we had shared this poem.

Beneath the Magnolia Tree

(for Edna St. Vincent Millay)

She was by the magnolia tree…
A dress, green, with large white buttons.
Her red (never carrot-colored) hair in a bun.
She was so young and beautiful,
Beneath the magnolia tree.

We talked, for a time,
The combined crimson and gold and platinum.
In the April afternoon
Beneath the magnolia tree.

I was six years her junior.
She would have people double that later in life.
We talked, her valentine mouth moving
Beneath the magnolia tree.

We both know how it ends.
I'm too young to stay,
She's too wild, but we press on
Beneath the magnolia tree.

Her dress has a hook at the top.
It unfastens easily, she sighs as it falls
Nothing but beauty beneath, as we embrace
Beneath the magnolia tree.

"Love is not all," we say,
As summer sings for a few moments
Beautiful, but temporary.
Beneath the magnolia tree.

Spring, summer, the death of autumn
Nears in the Hardy Garden.
Whose lips hers have kissed
And why, and where, I don't care,
As we lie innocent
Beneath the magnolia tree.

She moved on, as did I.
She would fade in later years,
From drinks and drugs and pain.
We would both forget when summer sang,
Beneath the magnolia tree.

The Summons

Arise! Arise. Oh poets of the Earth arise!
With ancient walls now crumbling
Our time again has come.

The fabric of life is frayed
And we the new loom must thread.

Gather minstrels and share the mysteries
Held deep within your soul
Commit to your labor
For birthing is upon us.

Warren Bellows

Fog

You are the music of silence
The thief of sight
And just the right pressure on skin

You divulge mysteries
Spider threads jeweled in pewter light

You shroud
Dissipate
And eddy back memories of lost dreams

Tonight I wander inside your world
Blinded by the simple joy of moisture

The Deep Search

If you want to unravel mysteries
Hiding inside of fog
Let your inquiry take you deep

If you want to know how energy creates particles and worlds of
    our own imaginings
Let your inquiry take you deep

Deep enough to remember sunlight embracing the arc of an orange
Deep enough to hear the chorus of crows
And whale songs
..... and ice melting away.

Deep enough to ask why?
And what happened?

                    And where are we now?

An Accounting

I am a stock in your portfolio
Acquired as a potential long term investment
Held now for 27 years
The dynamics of this acquisition have changed
You were never quite sure or enamored
But thought it might have some growth potential
Historically it has always underperformed
And now requires serious reevaluation

There were periods of growth
Increasing in value
It even yielded dividends for a time
But on the current balance sheet
It now jumps off the page
Bold red ink among a sea of black
A liability
One requiring constant attention and subsidy
No longer showing any possibility of upward mobility

Once a promising but more aptly just a comfortable investment
It smacks of declining financials
Poor operational policies
An infrastructure scattered and disorganized
One that is no longer forward thinking
A smart investor would have dumped it long ago
Perhaps blind loyalty or maybe nostalgia
Got in the way of sound investment practices

Now when life has begun accelerating
With the need to protect your financial future
You are jeopardizing your emotional one

As its major shareholder you do realize
The potential consequences of liquidating

Will the company survive
Is it destined for a long slow downward spiral
No longer recognizable
Or even listed somewhere
In case you are curious enough to check
Or need to assuage your feeling
About holding it too long

Somehow you became emotionally attached to it
Familiar to you
Always there among a list
Of constantly changing investments
To a person where change does not come easily
Sometimes you have to let go
In order to find out
There is still plenty of time
And other real possibilities
For an acquisition that is more suitable
To your current state of mind
Financial liking
Where the paradigm
Is more consistent with yours

Then there is always the possibility
Of holding on to this investment indefinitely
Displeased and full of angst
Wondering if this will be
just another one of your regrets

Jory Bellsey

The Last Stand

Fall nudges summer aside
In one swift move
And then it's gone
Hot steamy days and nights
Replaced by cool crisp ones
Once warm breezes have become
Chilling winds
A precursor of times ahead

However
Not everything is ready to yield
What was a full regiment of roses
Still has a dozen or so brave stems
Soldiering on
Defiant
Reaching skyward
In full regalia

A few remaining hydrangea
Stand guard at the driveway gate
Watchful and protective
Among their fallen brethren

Once a grandiose invitation
Welcoming all
Are now
Rigid and defensive
Their posture more deliberate and cautious
Heeding a warning

A lone clematis peeks out
Atop the trellis
A brimming wall of majestic purple
Has become a lone watchtower sentry
Waiting to announce the inevitable

And I too have come to realize
My summer
Has also passed
Uncertain now
How much fall remains
Before the challenges of winter
Set in

As I watch all the life around me
I stand upright
Alert
Ready
Wondering if it will be me
Who will be the last one standing

Service Dog

Dog, I said, in telegraphese, Dog,
what can you say? He looked at me
big brown eyes, pleading—don't they
all have this ability, to pull you in—
his muzzle white I assumed with age
and laid his head down on the carpet
with a sigh. His coat was covered

by another coat badged like a sheriff
in a Western, "Service Dog." He had
a lot on his mind, I could tell. Patience
or boredom, or a wish for diversion
from his responsibility for the man
sitting with buddies full of beer
and joviality after a game of handball.

I examined my motives. To extend
a friendly hand might elicit a whine of
recognition. Yet a compassionate gesture
could upset the balance. Dump us all, Dog,
me, those sweaty guys, practically the whole
messy world into a whirlpool of reactive
emotions. It was Sunday morning.

Many were at church but in this gym
we exercised our rights to recreation
rather than religion, thus a meditative
moment. It wouldn't last forever. Dog
closed his eyes. I dared not risk any
imagined outcomes, nor trust my own
perspectives, often shown up as false.

My groggy head sank down as Dog
raised his. Did he know a fellow beast
meriting more than desperation? Instant
messaging arrived from his direction
fighting past molecules of O_2, H_2O,
CO_2, pools of odorants: We help. We
care. Was a badge required? My master
approached. Help! I cried. Dog winked
and returned to dozing.

Christine Berardo

Living by the Sea

I've lived three weeks beside the sea.
Oblivious at first, I've come to recognize her moods.

Some days I wake to find her in a howling rage
throwing herself a fine old tantrum
against the impotent shore, furiously grinding
shells bits of wood small creatures plastic corks
pulverizing anything within reach into nothingness.
Fine white sand the residue of her fathomless fury.
She makes the air her co-conspirator
its winds screaming their wild dance
its rain spitting at my window
where I stand in awe, beholding her frenzy.

Other days she is a perfect lady.
Calm. Serene. Barely a ripple as she nibbles daintily
purring, lapping her wet tongue at earth's crusty edge.
Her placid Mona Lisa smile revealing nothing
of the dark, delicious secrets beneath her glossy surface.
A retinue of pelicans hovers over her
fans her brow in smooth feathered strokes
skims along her softly heaving body;
she sighs, yielding nothing.

But most days she's a restless cantankerous broad.
Tosses ceaselessly combing the banks as if
in futile search of something she's misplaced
a tantalizing thought perhaps
a word or snatch of melody that will not come
a bare fragment of dream that eludes, drives her nuts.
Back and forth she roams, muttering incessantly, scatters

out her discards onto sand, then gathers them back
to fling out another day along another shore.

She whispers to me in my sleep
awakens echoes from way back
the muffled roaring of the womb:
Diastole, systole. diastole, systole
mother-heart driving ebb and flow against
fetal eardrums, engraving tidal rhythms in conch and cranium
the saline taste of blood and flood
in every pore shell bone fiber fin skull scale cell

binding me in a universe of tissue, a universal issue
from the First Womb.
In my body pulse her lunar rhythms:
Ebb and flow——birth and death——low tide, high tide.
In my soul her watery depths: secrets
kept so dark they scuttle about
like blind bottom-dwelling larvae.
My mind, restless as mother sea herself,
roaming, sifting, churning up unsuspecting relics to the light
there to sort examine admire ignore
toss back on the outgoing tide for another time,
another perhaps distant shore.

Loose Magic

night falls dark
a day unspools
an undertow of exhaustion
closes the eyes

arriving in the middle
where all intrigue suspends
with tinkling bells the caravan of loose magic
rolls into town

bumping along an almost familiar road
scenarios swerve and sway
history no longer consigned to make sense
jars and slips from under the skin

landscapes conjured by perception
mind the subconscious
speak images in many registers
give wonder and irony the heave

the dead live again
permeate and linger
reveal the shape of wind
the dreamer is dreamed

for just this now
the curve of time does not exist
nor the buzz of endeavor
with its industry and sweep

somewhere a clock ALARMS
a surfeit of life will stir and forget
while the caravan of loose magic
heads off to its next destination

At Night

for Fran

in the dark I dream we dream together
our days generous with drama
we unload a dusty backstory

amid drift and mystery
our whirring parts of day
recede yet loom above a future

in the dark we dream
of reservoirs of good will
and pastel unending days

with sting and tenderness
how small an existence can feel
our story is a simple one
a blink of life in the dark

One Heart

I am alone,
surrounded by the laughter
of a hundred women
without menfolk or children

We have never met,
but we hug like sisters
swear like troopers
laugh like children
and speak the thousand intimate things
we cannot even tell our loved ones

The laughing voices swarm
around the puddles of light
like moths
while shy deer
stalk the shadows
with their tentative footsteps

Crickets throb—
the collective heart of our camp—
announcing our stories
of suffering and joy to the world
like a barker shouting,
Anonymity be damned!
Get your strength and hope here!
All the valleys and mountains
of a life beyond your wildest dreams
yours for the small price
of your experience,
your life as you know it
Cast your ego into the fire

and leap naked
into the arms of Spirit
where we are one woman
telling one story
from the heart

Houseguests

Houseguests—sick of 'em.
They gabble on
'til written words flee.

A mother duck hoards her babes, paddles
hard, drives them from indifferent
careless death.
So it must be with words,
for me.
They require a pocket of quiet,
shelter in the reeds
a gentle eddy,
a place to flock together,
grow.

Ward off houseguests
Invite words back, steer close, tend them
with time, small kindness, and tea.

Pondering Latte

Wiping the rim of my latte cup,
one of my gentle morning pleasures,
cleaning the edge of chocolate,
licking my finger,
sweet!

I sip while Trump one ups
Kim Jong-un, I sip while
storms swamp our generous world,
I sip while a Puerto Rican mom
begs meds for her infant son.

Here, in the capsule of
my morning quiet,
I try, and failing to hold it all,
sip—
and watch the sweet peas grow.

Becoming My Mother

As I grow old
I become more
my mother.
A curse some insist.
A blessing I reply
and the mirror shows
her large nose
gray hair
fine wrinkles.

A feminist before her time
she marched in protest
argued with the butcher
defended her children
magnified their virtues
whatever the cost.

She used to write
thank-you notes
in bold cursive
for every occasion.
Artificial I said then.
Necessary I see now.

She counseled
my friends
about losses and pleasures
ran my father's business
spoke loudly and often
but was known for her grace.

May I gain her soft strength
in coming days of conflict.

Laura Blatt

A Day of Rest

Begin at sunset
with challah and candles
dinner for two or more
praise on printed pages
a book of poems.

Turn off
phones
computers
all electronics
Turn up inner voice.

At sunrise enjoy
luscious strawberries
so sweet
so fragrant
in oatmeal with cream.

With sunshine and curiosity
observe the Goddess of
creeks and ferns
connect with heart
arrive at yet another sunset.

Stone Prayer

Stone, bone of Mother Earth—
Unwavering witness, sentinel, guardian of grief
Thank you for your sacrifice.
Your children kick pebbles, crush shells,
climb and mine mountains
while you stand silent—
carrying the burden of human sins
and well-intentioned achievements.

You were here first—
before I fell into time,
forgot my origin,
buried the breath of oneness.
You wait for me to remember
while you keep your vow,
Carving truth and courage
in my bones.
Grow the marrow to heal my human heart.
Invite miracles and synchronicity.
Guide me to live the life
you've sent to shine through me.

Jan Boddie

Giving Thanks

Receive, then give back.
Uniting the opposites
Feeds more than two souls.

Catharine Bramkamp

Patio Chairs

Behind the fence
Car doors slam like gun shots
Youths yell and strategize
over here, no, over there

The battle disturbs
this resident
Peeved at the racket she
hoists herself up to the fence
Peers over—ready to condemn
scold
lament what youth has come to.

She is too late
it's as quiet as No Man's Land

Across the cemetery
small American flags wave

Memorial Day

Reflections

The mirror's never been my friend
or hers,
or hers,
or hers.
Images glare back at us.
Traitors that we always trust—
annihilate and demonstrate
the parts of us we fear.

When did we learn to hate our curves
our bellies round
our full behinds?
Our psyches break with every bite
our confidence a wayward kite
that lifts then fractures
in the wind
under a broken sky.

Must we vomit
starve ourselves,
like models thin and movie stars
for us to feel desirable,
and sexily inspirable
in a society that holds regard
for a woman with no shape?

We promise to avoid the scales
become compelled, it never fails—
addicted like a ruthless sleuth,
the facts are clear
we hate the truth.
A simple pound can change the day
from joyful to despair.

Food is the enemy—
betrays us on mere sight.
Our warriors, drunk on pleasure,
have lost the will to fight.
An endless diet
That's our lives
Our futures fat and bleak.
Our appetites
bring switchblade thoughts
Why do we even eat?

Yellowtail Damselfish

(Microspathodon chrysurus)

What does an underwater creature know about
the night sky,
the stars in it?

Intense blue studded with diamonds,
a small fish flashes,
sliver of night sky cut from the galaxy's heart.

Juvenile Yellowtail Damselfish
Half the size of its name on the page.

A chance mutation chose night blue, the next one aimed
for the stars. Did the submarine sky struggle to reach
adulthood? An easy catch for predators, until one reduced its stars
    to dots
as it grew up—and reproduced. Yellow tail supplied further defense.

Absolute beauty had to become transient. A malevolent law,
cosmic balance—leave God out of this. Nature handles on her own.

Jewel Damsel
patrols its coral territory with the fervor of
a newborn star.

Tiny fish in improbable regalia blazing through muted surroundings
tangoing with my eyes.

Green eyes, ten deft fingers, four-chambered heart,
double circulation I have, yet not that blue,
those stars.

Monday Afternoon in West Marin

Black and white cows raise their heads to my car sailing by
Return to their banquet of grass
Like seals surfacing to check a boat
Then diving back down to fish.

Tomales Bay,
Shore of a sea of hills,
Winks in the sun.
Baby waves whisper
As they somersault on sand.

A bayside late lunch at the Marshall oyster farm:
Smoked trout afloat on puréed peas.
Guests swallow oysters and their briny bath
Voices ebb and flow
Shells crack.

I imagine stretching my interlude here
Into a life
Timed by tides.

The blue house on the bay is for sale
"Seafood Bar
BBQ Oysters
Dancing"
Painted on the side:
Life's essentials.

On the edge
Ocean of hills / bay
I exhale / inhale
Take it all in.

My Father on the Page

Once, out of the blue, my father,
my serious father, not given to excess,
not given to hyperbole, or metaphor,
said: I always thought I would grow up
to be a poet. No elaboration. No mention
of reading poetry in his youth.
Just that.

Years later, reading Wallace Stevens
for the first time, the entire opus
at one sitting, turning page after page
sitting on a small cot in our cottage
at Bread Loaf, in Vermont,
I remembered that moment.

My father a poet? What would it have
been like? What might he have written?
And then I knew why I was reading
Wallace Stevens, poem after poem,
hardly breathing between them, knowing
I was breathing them into my being,
into my brain, into my heart,
knowing for the first time in my life
my father on the page.

The Seventh Fear

Here on this holy ground
sanctified by your presence
      the music of the spheres
      woke me
      the shadow in Plato's cave
      gave me voice

I woke to the sound of the stream
      of no language
      and looked to the stars
      of no speech

Rescued from depravity
      dog fell to salvation
      and learned the power
      of happiness without fear
When the sun chose to rise
      dog gave up the bone
      of fear (as did I)
      and the seventh fear
      retreated to shadow

Speak to me of languages
      lost to the stars
            swallowed by black holes
      spoken only in the shadow
      of the moon struggling to rise
      stark against the mountain
            (that obsidian obelisk hiding the sun).

dog   freed from silence
speaks in sounds
        behind the tongue
        in sentences too ancient
                to be understood

Writer's Block

for Les

I know the shadow
of a poem
keeps you from writing

but shadows are full
of language
shrouded in mystery

and it is the mystery
you seek
always the shadowed

slanted, obscured view
of life
among the solitary

but when you feel
the music
of dissonance

is too much to bear
as the sun
shines on your reality

and you know
how temporary
the seasons of life are

you retreat to the cave
Plato engineered
to escape the poem

Annita Clark-Weaver

Moony

The men on the moon left footprints,
a flag, memory, and perhaps
a bit of DNA?

I rise early to watch the nearly full moon
hover on the western hill before
slowly sinking beyond my gaze.

Soon a fisherman in Juneau
will see her fall into the Gulf of Alaska
while a barefoot child in Tanzania waits

to see the moon come over the mountain
as I will do tonight when she is clothed
in her full glory of light.

We moon-watchers know each other
although we are not acquainted.
The moon abides.

Rebecca Del Rio

Under the Same Sun

Apart, we say, as a way
to soothe our separate souls,
"We're under the same moon."
Why not the same sun? The sun
whose light, too bright
cannot, will not shelter

or so we suppose. We chose
together, in so many languages,
the moon—softer, sweeter, it
smoothes the shadows. Still the sun
shines in broken Palestine and
Berlin at the same hour.

We shade our eyes, the luxury
of blinders, the refusal
to know what was caused,
In our name, what we allow.
We wait for the moon,
her soft absolution. Under

the same sun, we suffer
our simple losses, our separate
stupors. Our contours,
contrasts drawn sharp, certain,
so straight, we cannot
see how my soul touches,

reaches inside your body.
A soul, silver-sweet
as the moon, a body

radiant as the sun,
the one whose life
we live within and under.

The life we must bear
to know or burn together
in elected ignorance.

To Reiterate

To redo hone smooth make
perfect as best
as an old friend whom you
have lost touch with
by divorce, move, words
not said

To try again recast resay
rearrange
at best an exercise in
semantics—only the
canyon resounds with
whole-souled vowels of replay

To play as with blocks
to knock down rebuild
according to the written
constitution you carry within that
transfuses your actions
though unseen   misunderstood

To experiment work in
new mediums, clay, wood
used by the Incas to build —
kanchas roads and high
roads of stone, the grass-weaving
rope bridges arcing
crossing & recrossing valleys & gaps

To conceptualize   then
actualize

again and again   so what
the dead-cat bounce
under the stars—the
Big Dipper & Pleiades
still sparkle
to lignify the dead wood
to scrolls of meaning
an account of the best
of the worst the
gist of the day's play

Nancy Cavers Dougherty

Turn up the Thermostat

There should never
be cold hands on
summer days. Not
in emergency rooms
not in swaddle of
cotton on baby's skin.
Or the elderly's thin &
bruised skin.

But warm air
to leaven the faint
of heart, cultural
sway of the
medical ways—the
blue gloves, masks
beeps and charts.

Off the charts, the
ceaseless motion
of a multi-armed
monster, tattooed
in lotuses, deities &
semi-colons, to
deliver pills, inputs of
data to flesh
flesh to monitor. Screams.

Babble, piercings
anything to get
their notice, a kind word,
some lorna dunes

with water, gentle touch.
Gentle words of Rosa,
the only one to voice
"Are you all right,
lovey? There you are,
poor thing" to
elderly woman curled
in pain.

Her caring words castigating
the silence of all
the others, the RNs,
the NAs, the Jens,
thin-lipped Kerrys of
registration. Shattering
the nonchalance,
of scrubbed cover.

M. Justine Foster

Consequent

A tree lies in the water
 broken and dying
Uprooted from the sand

When last I saw it
It was tall
 and strong
With only bits of bare
 root showing

It was a long hard
 winter
The river tore at the
 shores
Slowly breaking soil
 away

Spring came with her
 floods
To soak the hard earth
 soft
Loosen surrounding
 stone

Then all it took
 was a gentle
 breeze
A whisper of wind
For the tree to come
 crashing
  down

Thank You

Thank you
for acquainting me
with the end
of parenthood.

Thank you
for stomping out of my life
in a flurry of invective
then remaining away.

Thank you
for reminding me
there is little left
for me to give.

Like a proper Zen master
wielding your stick
you've shattered my illusion
with well-aimed blows,

reminding me
of the futility of attachment,
the inevitability of pain.

I'm aware
all meetings
end with parting,
but I wasn't
expecting it
today.

Last month
the birdhouse
on the old pine
brimmed with activity,
then noise.
Now it's quiet,
empty.

Rachel Garcia

Translation

I watch for clues when dinner preparation begins. Ginger is sliced
into shingles, then pounded in a mortar to break it down into
a weeping sweet pulp. Peanuts are whacked; quick heavy thuds,
with a mallet, into uniform pieces. Lemongrass and garlic added
to hot oil. The sounds of this wild. Manic. A crowd roaring. Rice
noodles lay like resting snakes in a shallow basket, boiled with
vinegar to keep them white. This is a new language: fine juli-
enne instead of a pat on the hand, tightly wrapped spring roll for
We're just so happy to have you as a part of our family! The cut of
meat is important; I'll consider this equal to an heirloom teacup
passed down through world wars. I won't be gifted some womanly
treasure wrapped in a lace handkerchief, but I know to notice that
my piece of chicken isn't attached to a chicken foot. I see how she
slides the mint closer to me and pulls the Vietnamese coriander
away. I will take vinegar and oil and match-sticked cucumber and
call it love.

Rachel Garcia

Encyclopædia Britannica

I'm selling your books the ones ordered through a subscription
which came once a month one by one spanning my childhood the
collection grew as did I (I'm sorry I tried not to) then no one read
books anymore

there's a page bookmarked with your race tag #144 from the day
you ran and ran and your nipples bled because you forgot to tape
them then

spent hours in the bath and I was allowed to look at you soaking

"the nature of light" is waves or velocity or electrostatic things
moving fast something I see but prefer to believe just comes from
a light switch in your room that stays off

The Lurking Lace

The shoelace lurked
The old man, unaware
Needing to do something
Twenty yards from there
Just a hop over the conveyer
An easy thing to do
Unless, I guess, you're in
The middle of year 62
The guys I work with
Are all half my age
Forgetting that, sometimes
Not really acting the sage
Over the conveyer
With a little grace Except for the shoe
With that lurking lace
Reaching out and grabbing
The grippers, it did
Not gonna be pretty for my ego or my id
Bottom line here I scraped skin off my shin
Looking all the old man I didn't make a sound
Screaming on the inside
But outside not out loud
Walk to the first aid kit
Walk like nothing's wrong
Slap some Band-Aids on it
The pain won't last long
With flesh tone Band-Aids
Blood leaking past
Think no one will notice
As retirement approaches fast

Susan Gunter

At the Bulgarian Natural History Museum

We climb dark stairs past moth-eaten animals
so long dead they no longer frighten,
past cages with cracked panes full of snakes—
two boas in one, in another a coral that had shed
its skin in a transparent shimmery whole.

This is the natural history museum?
I can't decipher the dim cyrillic signs,
though I spent two months making
flash cards for each letter of the alphabet.

We reach the top, a Nabokovian dream:
drawer after drawer of Purple Emperors,
Grass Jewels, Phalakron Blues, Coppers.
I have tried to make my life as ordered
as these butterflies in their dusty cases.

But my middle son was hit, damaged—
he twenty-five, come here to mend
in this broken country, me running near
him with a net to scoop him and pin him
down if he falters, to record his losses
on three by five cards and file them
in wooden boxes in alphabetical order—
but it doesn't seem enough.

Failure to love: that might come under
the last roman numeral in my outline
when I write about this.

Qi-Gong

The simplicity of the tantean breath, the gentleness
of the movements coming from the body into
warm still air, the absolute need to do nothing but
breathe, breathe, breathe while the mind retreats
to a point three fingers below the belly button and stays
there, immobile and attentive. The arms move in slow
rhythm while the breath propels the body up, down.
No images form. No stray thoughts come. This is all
we have, all we want: control over desire, chaos.

I wrote this poem the same way, lulled into word silence
while my mind did its work without my knowing.

Roadhead

*The ocellaris clownfish lives among the tentacles of certain sea anemones,
secreting a mucus that protects it from being stung.*

Come down to the trampled meadow where await
the vehicles abandoned here last week,
at the brink of the gone world.

Exhaling, shed the elemental load
of shelter, clothing, and what's left of the food.
The mountain rising like a shoulderblade
has seen the back of you.

Reenter the land where it is all allowed:
to bathe in purchased water, read by light
that has been miles in copper, feel again
the vigilance of commerce on the skin
and feel your weapons changing:
who tomorrow shall be known
not for your compass-work or skill with fire
but by the name of whom you serve,
by the strength of whom you hire.

No, it is not corruption, to come down.
But what is this small stiffening within?

What is this tremor as you feel it close:
comfort: the trap in which we learn to live
as does inside the pale and petaled mouth
the small gold fish that is not stung, but feeds.

Façade

How fragile
how embedded
our façades
sift
sliding one to another
a blip of moment
a slight memory
a glancing blow
put on a half-smile to shield
a snapshot that would bring us to our knees
no scrutinizing here
nor do we rage or break
we keep moving
if slowly
so as not to be ensnared
hiding from ourselves
let us not wallow
let us not revisit
we draw the curtain of all right tighter
so no one's piercing light
may shine in

Fuzzy white rock
through window

sorry I am
for your loss
expense
inconvenience
in the nippy days that followed

while aim was true
I did not intend
to cause you pain

oh, but how
shiny
were the shards
in the afternoon sun
exploding like fireworks
for me

Slanted

Tile floor
cold
sitting
counting the nothingness
this is my drop of blood
what say you

I will talk anyhow
my voice does not need you
it is valid

these white walls
have seen worse than I

apathetic I am
but I care enough
no label branded far too early
will hold
I shred it
become … other

I hold many aspects
what is your perspective
take a title I prefer
wear tarnished crown
let others crow
they have not my voice
    I am not for everyone

I whisper
whimper

silent
shout
live within these mottled walls
claim them mine

as windows
I climb through

OUT OF SILENCE 77

Pamela Heck

Because of you

I woke today
considering the nuances
of "longing" versus "wanting,"
calculating length and breadth
and pondering
at just what point
"want" turns long.

There is an immediacy to wanting.
Longing lingers,
reeks of regret,
replaces *now* with *then,*
or looks ahead with trepidation.

Set aside longing.
It is a wet blanket
to be shaken and dried,
cut up,
tucked away in drawers—
sachet of sweet remembrance
to be sniffed from time to time,
not imbibed.

I do not want,
and seldom long for,
what has passed,
but will reflect,
from time to time,
on what was gained
and what was lost
because of you.

Prayer for Dying

this massive darkness
beckons me, welcomes me
and I welcome it

every day, let me see the light from the window
shining into my room
throwing shadow and shapes on the floor

but at night, don't cover the window
let me eat the darkness
let it seep into the room
let it melt into my open arms
and make me one with eternal rest

Barbara Hirschfeld

Home of Ancient Wisdom

The jangle of the day's commotion
recedes with the opening of the door
to the darkened room
    candles lit
    cushions in place
    stepping stones in the midst
    of the river's rush

Water slips over marbled rock
as easily as loose garbage
swirls across the pavement
in New York
twisting in a tortured wind
the mind cannot gain a foothold.

I sit down.

Sweet smelling incense grounds me here
Sun shadows lean into the woven rug

in my sanctuary

I dip my ladle
into the sacred
liquid
of open space

Seaside

Rare sunny morn
we hear the birds
rejoice in song
and watch above
as they perform
their random blue ballet

Along the shore
to thrum of waves
that crash and fan,
we analyze
the salty clues
they scrawl

We walk,
deciphering our lives
till fog wraps cliffs
in wispy shrouds

We leave unclear
yet reassured
by the gifts
of repetition

Louise Hofmeister

The Avian Way

I watch you as you
tilt and hold, flap and lift
I marvel while you dive and drift—

are you merely on your way?

Go ahead and preen your preen
crane your neck, stretch your beak
Warble, cackle, trill and shriek—

do you know you're on display?

From here, in these my waning days,
as I stop to listen, stare or glance
at your abundant song and dance—

I'm pretty sure it's safe to say
that you've become the way I pray.

The Airborne Sea

Around a curve
a sudden change
as sea ghosts rush
in exodus

An unkempt band
that blacks the sun
while softening
darker spaces

Wind-driven
river-lured,
the raucous hoard
stampedes

And in its wake
an eerie scene
a world transformed,
all blurred around the frame

I park, take stock
becalmed by grey
and raise my
teaming mind
to a softer, wider plane

Natosi Johanna

Mutilated Praise

based on Adam Zagajewski's *"Try to Praise the Mutilated World"*

Try to praise the mutilated world,
Difficult terrain, I know.
Earth's wounds are my wounds,
Earth's heart wars mine as well.

Remember this is not metaphor
Meant to appease the poetic.
Remember this is real, solid science
Meant to rattle your maiming chains.
You must praise the mutilated world

Or else face the mutilation
In the mirror. *You watched* the waters
Grow dankly dark. *You've seen* polar bears
Slip into oblivion. *You've heard* the lion's
Roaring silence. You should…

You should praise the mutilated world.
Praise—*Remember* this world is home,
                    poisoned or not.
Praise—*Return* in thought to eternally evolving
                    cleansing.
Praise—*and* in praising, the mangling shreds
                    will skin together.
Praise—*and* in praising, wholeness will meld
                    Earth into one.

Praise the mutilated world—
Love swirls InOut and returns.

NOTE: Zagajewski's words are italicized in the body of the poem.

Natosi Johanna

I of Zen

I
dive deep
into my murky abyss—

    the resting place
    for thought not realized
    for thought spliced
    for thought not
    thought

    the rusting place
    for dreams not actualized
    for dreams broken
    for dreams not
    dreamt

I
scour the walls
of this bottomless cauldron
sludge incessantly
rising to my mind's edge

I
dip a finger
into the foam
raise it to my lips

I
blow the dust
back
to my stars

Natosi Johanna

when i get old

when i get get old,
i won't need poetry
anymore.

crafted, pretty words
have been crushed by
ways of becoming
unknown before.

no sonnet, villanelle,
limerick, or slam
can out-voice the
insight of age.

the simile has died.
the metaphor is literalized.

the beat rings silent
pulsing between soul-ular shells—
seaskins that know
the big bang.

driven by dreams once
haunting my days,
the graceful carriage
approaching
is my only pregnant
pause.

  In the meantime,
  life is an elephant.

James Kelly

AIR WAR

I am dead now
Somehow having never lived
Or loved

We are told by politicians in great ceremonies
Amid the crash of crowds and colors
We died protecting freedom
From the splash of rolling childrens' tears

I don't recall the cause so just
But I do remember
Beneath the din of screaming blades
Hearing cries of mothers lost in war
Torn from their babies by
Silver knives dancing
On midnight moonbeams
Of foreign skies

Shastina

A river bends and unbends, scattering light
On the way to briny waters
Following turns of earth's rough surface
Carving out its own shape
Long before the simmering cone lifts sky's blue edge
The river coursing draws life to its elemental sound

A crater rises, magma gathers, until a widening rush of sound
Erupts the volcano's hot liquid light
Dredging a canyon from the western edge
Time, over a windfall of seed and water
Pours a forest along its shape
Rain fills basins in the pocked surface

Pines bristle as breezes surface
Birds, with their arcs of sound
Move through trees according to their shape
Empty-boned, feather-light
Hearing food smelling water
Dive to the pond's forested edges

A frog, squatting at mud's uncertain edge,
Tastes air from the moving surface
Reflections shift in rumpled water
And the absence of sound
In oblong patterns of dusty light
Signals the presence of danger, swift by its shape

The frog, assuming stealthy shape
Watches the shallow's greening edge
Midges blink in and out of striped light
Striders skitter the surface
A hollowed log fattening the roundfull sound
Of mating calls from across the waters

Tadpoles scatter in algae under water
Small darting tapered shapes
Drop blunt dampened sounds
Hunt the uneven edge
Sharp pecks wrinkle the surface
Nipping at bugs that alight

The settling sun drains the final light
From water's witnessing surface
Its round soundless shape falls over day's slow edge.

Doran Beach

Winds riff sand into folds
Small shorebirds nestle in the dunes
Twisted cypress interrupt the wind
That blows into fog

Twisted cypress interrupt the wind
Wind that fetches distant waves
Blows into fog
Early morning slips the tide away

Wind fetches waves
Unsettling driftwood in spurts and rolls
Early morning slips away
Crabs crawl slideways in the wash

Unsettling driftwood
Southward currents heap knobs of shell and tangle
Crabs crawl tidewise
Large brown birds parallel morning skies, orange pouches slack

Southward currents heap knobs
Bourne in bitter kelp forests holding fast in deeper waters
Large brown birds parallel morning skies
Circling wing shadows stir the fish

Borne in bitter kelp forests holding fast
Flashy half-grown rockfish lull in shifting curves of green
Circling wing shadows stir
Seaweed loops and turns
Flashy half-grown rockfish lull in briny curves
Past smells of wet sand, beyond foam of breaking waves
Seaweed loops and turns
Beaks hunt the churn, black ducks clatter lines of dark water

Past smells of wet sand, beyond breaking waves
Slack water marks the changing tide
Black ducks clack in dark water
Particles of light murmuring the surface turn to waves

Slack water marks the change
Drifting south in zig zag currents
Particles of light murmur the surface
Small white birds with angled wings dive

Drifting south in zig zags
Salt air bows the rasping call of gulls
Small white birds dive
Rowdy furrows of ebbing sea

Salt air bows the call of gulls
Skinny-beaked rummagers skitter
Rowdy ebbing furrows
Muddling the sand

Skinny-beaked skitterers rummage
Tending the fractal shore
Muddling the sand
Long-leg birds chase water's rogue edge

Tending the shore
Beach Hopper bubbles pock the wake
Quickstep birds chase water's edge
Sun bends orange light over the ocean

Bubbles pock the wake
Winds fold sand
Sun bends orange light
A shorebird
Nestles the dunes

Briahn Kelly-Brennan

Day Long Strut Song

Barking out a quick quack
Crowing to the peck pack
    Hopping from her sit site
Chasing down a bit bite
    A bit bite

Hey Chicken Chicken
Eat Another Bug

Pecking at a slug snag
Stooping for a grub grab
    Snacking in the dill dell
'Til she has her fill full
    Her fill full

Hey Chicken Chicken
Eat Another Bug

Strutting with a flip flap
Dozing in a snap nap
    Jumping on a stump step
Poking with a pick peck
    A pick peck

Hey Chicken Chicken
Eat Another Bug

Following the sun signs
Homing to her pin pine
    Slowing when the sun's done

Roosting with her hen hon
   A bit bite
      Her fill full
     A pick peck
         Her hen hon

Hey Chicken Chicken
Eat Another Bug

Elizabeth Klein

What if No One Comes

Every so often, I count how many friends would actually come to my funeral. It would be so embarrassing if only a handful showed up. A friend and I joke about this now and then. Recently I said *this would be a good time for me to call it quits, I have a nice crowd right now.*

For my 60th, my brother gave me a surprise party. He had a hard time rounding up enough people to come. My friends didn't all know each other, several didn't live close anymore. He invited neighbors I barely ever spoke with. I knew they didn't want to come but felt it unkind to say no. They brought a tiny red ashtray as a gift. Some people traveled an hour to get there. I was so embarrassed I could barely speak, especially since we didn't have much to offer. Dinner was over, it was simply birthday cake and drinks.

Maybe that's why I'm so taken by this recent grave in the nearby cemetery, a rectangle of three by seven feet of large river rocks —large enough to hold in one's hand. A one-word description written on each: Resplendent, Principled, Discerning, Dauntless, Quick-witted, Engaging, Insecure, Picky, Short Tempered, Contradictory, Had hoped for more…
Was afraid no one would come.

Christopher Layton

Man's Industry

From quarries and mines dug deep by man
Rainforests of Brazil
Lapland's icy Arctic grip
Italy's warm skies

Huge trucks crawl like ants
Gigantic cutting wheels
Immense thrusting arms
Cutting stone, back and forth
Back and forth, back and forth

Dwarfed men controlling
Steel yokes with diamond teeth
Slashing ageless granite
Gushing water sprays tortured stone
Cooling hot steel blades
All shadow beneath smoky blue arc lights

Monster blocks give up their gems
Slabs sparkle and wait in disarray
Frozen treasures in stone
From Carrara, Italy and beyond

Roger C. Lubeck

Cacophony

A forest is never silent.
We journey deep into Nature's green heart
Searching for that elusive moment of quiet and solitude.
We seek a peace that doesn't exist.

A forest is never silent.
When a tree falls, does it make a sound if we are not there to hear?
Of course it does. How preposterous.
A forest is alive. It exists without us.

A forest is never silent.
Leaves tap out a cypher from the wind
Birds twill a melody of love. Squirrels scold and chatter.
Bugs, flies, and bees add white noise to Natures' cacophony

A forest is never silent.
It roars at us until all thought is driven from our brain.
In that absence. In our loss of self.
There is solitude.

Donald Mackay

From Where He Stood

He carved in wood the shapes of seals and birds
As he sat just outside his cabin door
Their barks and cries were music that he heard
One day he chose to quiet the singing shore
When small he used to take us in his clanking van
To walk the cliffs above the crescent beach
Once scared I took his giant hairy hand
That never—ever—went too far from reach
They say he used to drink more than his share,
And time went by so we'd all grown and gone
His brother found him hanging quietly there
He'd left a note to tell him what he'd done
"Do not despair or grieve at such a loss
I'm free from bottle there, no mind the cost!"

Ana Manwaring

Arguments in Favor of a Happy Marriage in No Particular Order

1.
In the monster hours,
your mind a crucible churning—
your spouse's snores soothe.

2.
He loves cats, she loves dogs
together you adopt a menagerie
of furry love.

3.
One of you knows how to mow
one of you knows how to prune
you both can grill a steak.

4.
Your children grow up leave home,
eventually follow in your footsteps
resulting in grandchildren.

5.
Rising prices, the market a bear,
home values falling and retirement on the horizon.
Two incomes are better than one.

6.
Across the breakfast table a smile and news.
Forgotten last night's argument—
a new day and no fault.

7.
When you're invited to a ball
you pull your wedding dress and tux from mothballs—
you're good to go.

8.
Men generate heat while women shiver
(until a certain age) lots of snuggling
turns temperate your atmosphere.

9.
Life looks rosier when you've
someone to care for. And you've
got an excuse to go home.

10.
You'll always have a friend to attend
that new film, play, concert, game, lecture,
or traffic court.

11.
No matter how wild and impossible your dreams,
your spouse will rein you in
or egg you on.

12.
If you're one prone to loneliness
you'll always have someone
to be lonely with.

13.
A happy marriage—a happy life. It's true,
the institution will change you,
but it's better than the alternative.

Ana Manwaring

Stone Corral Creek Breaches Banks

Maxwell, CA 2/20/17

No one outside town seems to care
Swift's Stone Corral is flooded and closed,
swamped from history.
The swollen land can't take any more rain
after so long without.

At two a call, "bring the boat, the creek's spilled over."
Eleven hundred three souls evacuated
ferried to hills beyond the rain swelled
rice paddies, to watch through graying dawn
the crop swept along the current.
Men waded from the Old Maxwell Saloon,
helped to shutter and sandbag.
These, the almond farmers,
watched as rain pelted early blossoms
to soggy ground.

Stone Corral Creek Breaches Banks
A tiny farming town washes in muddy run-off:
a river of pesticides and fertilizers and farm debris.
In three hundred-sixty five homes
the folk pack their soggy possessions,
load into the rescue boats and drift
across their fields, washing up
like flotsam onto higher shores.

Laura McHale Holland

My Grandmother's Flat

my grandmother's flat
dusty, musty
soot on the radiator
a dungeon to eyes
that cannot see beyond
cracked fixtures
that tell of a woman
who limps like a bird
shot down
but survives, hidden
from hounds on the hunt

my grandmother's flat
full of hats in greens
lavenders, blues
all pastels, shelved now
remnants of Easters past

tarnished silver craving
her touch, weeping
in velvet-lined case
creaking boards
creaking bones
my grandmother's flat
where concrete holds
patches of grass
like bars of a jail

all this falling apart
this sorrow, all this soot
this quiet, waiting
listening for death

yet my grandmother's flat
woos and cradles all who enter
her sons, granddaughters
ghosts of people long gone

we all will move on
yet remain here too
in my grandmother's flat

Artists' Lineage

Gray-black bird, slick and small,
lifeless among those leaves
the live oak drops during spring rains.
Still supple to my foot. To my hand
a puppet animated from below
by maggots relishing it.

Child poet, will you
parent the adult?

Like Camille Pisarro, born and raised under Flamboyant
trees in Saint Thomas. Painting away his waning years,
among hayfields and apple trees in Éragny, France.

      Two women in homespun bend to pick up apples,
      a third observes, while a man shakes the tree.
      The curve of Earth written on the field in rows,
      procession of oaks along the crest. Points of light and dark,
      wheeling swirl of yellow green brown pink purple.
      Contained in a gold frame.

"When did you *stop* being a poet?" William Stafford
asked the interviewer. (I will keep writing.) Van Gogh said,
"If you hear a voice within you say *you cannot paint,*
then by all means paint, and that voice will be silenced."

Neighbor field explodes with small green pennants of oats,
purple and white petals of wild radish.
An apple tree bends under the beauty
of its pink-white blossoms.

Tubes of paint are pages of the thesaurus.
Brush strokes are words.
Pointillists use short words.

Funny how doves here speak
exactly the same dialect as ones in France.
I will keep writing.

Ghosts*

*And when he that doth flee unto one of those cities shall stand
at the entering of the gate … and shall declare his cause in the
ears of the elders …, they shall take him … unto them, and
give him a place, that he may dwell among them. Joshua 20:4*

After fifty years I return.
In my school days, I didn't hear them.

Not Pastor Trocmé breathing courage
into his flock. *Trust God for daily bread.*
Share said bread with brothers, sisters.
Resist with weapons of the spirit.
Stone temple, wooden beams and cross.
Whitewashed walls. Clear windows full of leaves.

Not Magda cycling hard to "House of Stones" School
defending one student from Gestapo.
He had saved a German from drowning.
                    The others had no such excuse.

Not the farmer who rented out a room,   gave cover to forgers,
cranking out 50 sets of false papers each week.

Not the middle-aged Jews dressed in Boy Scout shorts
led by a teen   through French woods to   Swiss woods.

Not the town doctor   who pleaded release for two prisoners
was then   himself   butchered   in Lyon.

Not the residents of the mass grave
        in the place since known as German Woods.

Not Villon's "Ballad of the Hanged Men" enacted by a visiting
   troupe.
Young Jean-Pierre Trocmé, the pastor's son, tried a noose around
   his neck
to see   how it would feel   slipped, died
Father   forever   blamed   himself

*The populations of le Chambon-sur-Lignon and other villages of the Haute-Loire
were honored as Righteous Among Nations in 1990 by the Yad Vashem Institute
in Jerusalem for their role in sheltering Jews and helping them escape during World
War II.

Phyllis Meshulam

Chapel

in the Dordogne

The cave entrance looks like a distant
crystal ball predicting our present, perhaps
our future. The cave is our ancient past.

A cavalcade of bison and deer as vivid as
a projection, in ochres, reds, blacks on white
limestone. Fleeting mane of horse, spine of rock.
Revived from their grave by a wand of light.

Four boys on a lark in the woods in 1940,
many worlds away from Vichy, Paris, Berlin.
They followed their nosy dog, who broke through
a clay seal to 20,000-year-old buried treasure.

For the artists was it a lark? A sacred mission?
To revere and celebrate the lives that sustained
theirs, as Eskimo hunting songs
thank and beguile hoped-for prey?

Women and men, evidence suggests.
Six artists working with minerals
loosened by animal fat, textured with
ground bone. Expert prehistoric palette.

The red reindeer licks the face of the black one
which bows down, bends its knees. I ask,
"Had they locked horns? Was one submitting?"
"It is a love story," the guide replied. "And war
was not invented until the time of domestication."
Weak in the knees for love.
Womb of cave birthing more bison, horses, deer.

This Sistine chapel. In its zone, I think I feel its
Michelangela, Raphael.

Gathering Time

I.

Eleven years old, an overnight with Grandmother,
alone with the guest bathroom mirror and the polished tile

where a slender vase holds pale-gold stalks of rattlesnake grass,
each transparent seed an unborn plant, tied by a fragile thread.

Newly widowed, Grandmother went to Asilomar,
walked in the pine grove and gathered a handful of rattlesnake grass,

I think her souvenir's exotic. Just a weed along the coast,
rattlesnake grass didn't grow anywhere near our inland ranch.

II.

Thirty-two years old, at Grandmother's burial,
a dozen Dutch iris lie across my lap.

Her favorite hymn ends the service, then I lay
the blue iris down with the formal bouquets.

Fifty-two years old, on the road to the Lifeboat Station,
I pluck a handful of rattlesnake grass from the crumbling slope,

leaving the Douglas iris blooms to fade away here
in their native soil, remembering the stories,

how collectors come to dig up roots,
maybe to sell, maybe to plant in gardens.

I don't know which story is true.

III.

Three years old, I walk through the cow pasture
behind our house in Agoura, wild oats stand up stiff,

hide me in a narrow canyon of pale straw,
I hear a rattle, see a snake coiled in my trail.

Turn, now, go back.

IV.

Dead, I think, holding stalks of rattlesnake grass,
hard to believe I killed this, tore it from the earth, roots and all,

living grass that stood among the newly-risen iris.

What I don't know could fill a ravine—
how the people of these hills named the native flowers,

if they used the roots, or found them bitter poison,
how they wove baskets with last year's dried leaves,

what stories they told their grandchildren
when they saw the year's first growth on the hills,

if their songs rattled like grass in the wind.

V.

Above the Estero waters, sun-bleached grasses cluster,
memories gather like roots pulled from hillsides,

a resurrection of uncertain meanings,
anchored by nothing more solid than scattered seeds,

and the language of leaf upon leaf.

Upon a Stone

I want to catch my foot—
I want to stand
among the oldest stones,
polished, slick with time,
carved by that restless sculptor,
water traveling down canyon—

I want my footprint to remain
the way those former residents,
duckbills and stegosaurs,
left a mark upon a salty shore
for coal miners to uncover
suspended from a tunnel ceiling;

I'll gather my heaviest thoughts,
press down and leave something
even blackrock can't ignore.

Clare Morris

A Charmed Life

I am a royal refugee
my begging bowl
an invisible cup

My privilege
a long shadow
shape of my poverty

Patricia Nelson

The Loved

Love shapes the loved
with the white, awed silence on its hands.
It does not lift the wide and faulty
to its narrow eye.

Does not admit
the common or the small
when sun makes sharp the till
on the bright edge of a face.

On, love is brighter than a water spider
rare and blue and sunlit on a skin of image.
It is thin and long in its stepping,
a shimmer of stepping.

The loved is quiet in its bead of light,
is a stillness of glass.
Is loved without banging or breakage.
Is loved only.

Brigid

Brigid was a goddess of sky and weather in pre-Christian Ireland. She was the patron of poetry, sacred wells, and early spring, as well as sacred flame. Her festival day, Imbolc, was a time to predict weather. She invented keening, a mourning combination of weeping and singing, and a whistle used for night travel.

i.
We land small and ignorant
and with a magic whistle
at the bottom of the night sky,
the animal hour alive in all its furs.

The land we see by day
is the weighted land of words,
bouldered, carved, and hard.
Sky in its purse of rain is heavy, black with song.

It holds our twisting ears against a vastness,
shows the dumbstruck
all the tricks and cracks of light,
beats its iron bell in the dark.

ii.
We come to storm or flower
as we must: wild, untuned.
We pray to stars and weathers:
to all turning stones that hang and burn.

We crave the gentle goddess
complicit in our music and our mourning,
awake to the rolling equinox of home
with its temporary birds and candle-bright rain.

She who keens, in a height, our loves,
our losses, the demons that we dream.
She folds the sky for us,
absolves with spring the numerous and small.

Our unkempt singing holds her stillness,
her weathers, her poets' curving apples
picked from the tall, traveling fires
with long and grieving hands.

The Mountain Roars

In Dante's Purgatorio, sinners climb a mountain as they atone for their sins. The mountain shakes with joy when they finally expiate the sins.

It is more than the tissue of air,
the revelations coming, color by silent color,
to those with light on their faces.

So much more than a border marked
by a door, a stair, or a secret
gliding in a green and weightless dusk.

There is stillness. Those at the final gate
look up, having expiated everything.
They rest their feet on the last shadow.

There is sound. The mountain moves
its loud and interlocking rocks,
booms as they leave time.

Its seams sing everywhere,
open dark and downward beaks,
speak each white incidental wing and fall of water.

It knows, the mountain that hurt them as they climbed,
that shook the heaped, imperfect hinges
of their bones and their beliefs.

It roars joy as they exceed the metaphor:
the shape of mountain, the clean first hour as a human,
the always-leaning castle of atonement.

Michael O'Brien

life bending

beneath the weight
of sunshine and of dark
nights. of rains on long grasses.
the weight of no rain, of gray hunger.
the weight of pain. the weight of water from
glaciers melting. the weight of dead brothers, sadness
of sisters, missing mothers and fathers. the weight of full
pockets and of empty minds. the weight of refugees in boats

Michael O'Brien

Gravity

"The earth is pulling you straight down but the Sun is
pulling you straight up." Tahir Yaqoob, *Exoplanets and
Alien Solar Systems*

pulled from
either end—
do you read
the news again or
write crisp poems?

but as neighbors spy
schools interrogate
and soldiers hold
rifles on tanks rolling
down your road

the news becomes
personal
writing poems
suddenly endangers
your quiet

your quiet home
your wife
your children all
pulled from
either end

Michael O'Brien

from syria

the child's
dark-rimmed
eyes aged and
war-weary

young soldier's face
as he kneels
before the child
hugging him

both with loving
mothers and fathers
who could not soften
the nightmares

of bombed buildings
and bodies,
damaging the spirit
already haunted

soldier holding
in this child a version
of himself as he was
but cannot know

the nightmares to come
from the guilt of
his own children
safely tucked into bed

of a house with food
and laughter and
of sometimes peace with
kisses good-night—

this young soldier
who will some day
write poems but
not find his words

Jan Ogren

Life Dreams Itself

I had a dream
then my dream had a dream
composing images, designing, deciding

forming me, forming you

then that dream had a dream

established our relationship, organized our lives
bought a house, had children
developed careers
one moment after another, blending harmonizing,

then that dream had a dream—

reconstructed me, reconstructed you
envisioned grandchildren
new experiences,

made sense of my world

so that I understood it all,
had it all placed
arranged, known.
Day by day, building on itself.

then that dream had a dream.

Renelaine Pfister

Playing in the Rain

The heavens grumble
It starts to drizzle
We yelp with pleasure
Take off our clothes
Run outside in our underwear

Heavens pour
Joy pours out of our hearts
Nothing could be better
Than the beat of rain on our bodies
Soaking us, embracing us, baptizing us

We dance in the ran
Splash in the puddles
Worship the water pouring down
We cup our hands to collect it
We open our mouths
to taste it

This was when
we knew what happiness was
That if happiness were tangible
we were holding it in our hands
We wish to freeze that time
Preserve it in a vessel
That will never wear out or be broken

We're no longer kids
It rains outside
And we stay indoors
We want the rain to end

We've lost the wonder
We are weary
We no longer laugh
Or play

Ellie Portner

Blue Butterflies

A butterfly flew into the house
Through an open door
Its translucent wings
The blue of the Seagram's
Crown Royal whiskey bag
Gramma Fanny
Had gifted my child-self
My fingertips remember
Touching the soft velvet
The machined yellow embroidery
Pulling the draw strings tight
To keep my few coins safe inside

I raised an open hand
To the lost butterfly
Offering it a resting place
Hoping I might feel the vibrations
Of its weightless energy
On the palm of my hand

Hurry little flyer I called
As it flew back out the door
Your time is shorter than mine
The blue butterfly was gone

My traveler-self
Remembered buying
A butterfly barrette in China
It's fluttering metal wings
Threaded with blue beads
…I clipped it in my hair

In my myth-self
I am a bearer of butterflies
A holder of heaven
An earthbound wanderer
In search of Art's truth and intention
In my myth-self … I am content

Forward/Backward

I intended to write a comeback poem
this past year a blur, though
and now, that awful expected
stare backwards

did I have an assignment?

the ring of those silent yellow walls
echoing with new plots
of no real use but hanging, accumulated

out the window, past the bamboo shoots
is a place I go when I've stopped looking at you
or the Swedish office chair or small Chinese paintings
red oriental rug bunched under my feet

why did I come back?

The image of orange-breasted birds returning
to my backyard feeder won't leave me
someone remembers to put food out
holds them in mind
does not care
where they've been.

Harry Reid

The Greening of the Earth

The Greening of the Earth comes sly
Without a Word, and one Forgets
That Winter's disregard slipped by,
As Snow turned into Rivulets.
In the Flutter of the Swallow,
The Convening of the Wren,
And in the Pussy-Willow
In every Wood and Fen,
It Often comes to us Unseen,
The Turning of the Earth to Green

Linda Loveland Reid

Misadventures of Venus and Mars

I. **First Love**
   Desire spins fast,
   At the rate of love.
   Life whirls circles into squares,
   Boxes holding in the ache.

II. **Mating Season**
   Vonnegut-wit, about him they'd say.
   So she thought for some hours and all through the week.
   Whitmanesque she decided at length would last,
   At least until May and leave her a past.

III. **Relationship**
   "Full frontal honesty,"
      he said that I said.
   "Beyond boggling stupid,"
      I said that he did.

IV. **Re-beginning**
   A kitchen table is forever,
   Moments on and on.
   Sugar settles on the stomach,
   Like lying on the tongue.
   She cannot tell of long past matters,
   Secrets of a life gone wrong.

Autumn

Once rushing to tumble from its border,
A lone red tomato clings to its limp vine,
A few green balls, done, refusing to ripen.
Nature's energy is on hold,
hesitates, is waiting.
Eager green drains to the vibrant of amber and red.

The resting season is upon us,
no longer thrilled by the flutter of butterflies.
I can now only imagine the peach smell of a rose.

The crispness of cerulean blue floats above.
Soon there will be an unseen something,
the eye of a blackbird against the winter snow.
I breathe in the feeling of orange,
Of beauty-on-a-binge.
Autumn is about letting go.

Lighter Load

Porsche was a hundred pounds of
Love, friendship, security, and fur.
Four paws, a long wet nose, tall alert ears,
A tail that reached the floor and more.
Snaggle-toothed and smiling, a pure German Shepherd.

A gentle giant who intimidated the mailman
Behind windows at the front door.
Spinning, barking, neck hair standing on end.
UPS—the rumbling brown box—got the royal treatment.
Porsche resembled a police dog with a cornered suspect.

Children loved to pet the black-faced scary-looking dog
Who licked their hands and wagged her tail
As they dug their fingers in her long, thick hair.
Only the bravest wanted to pet her head—so
Close to those big ugly teeth.

She joined our family at four months old.
Sleek and black with hints her fur would lighten,
She knew when she arrived she'd found her family.
Awestruck by her size and kindness,
Everyone loved her.

Vet bills quickly began to accumulate.
In the exam room, blood and puss dripped from her nose.
The vet smiled gently at me—not a brain tumor.
An abscess had ruptured above a top tooth.
Once extracted, the space invited a free-for-all.

Porsche came with us to Sonoma County at age two.
One month earlier, we lost the Shepherd before her
Whom Porsche had adopted as Mama for a year and a half.
In front of clothes and linens packed in the way-back,
Porsche traveled well on the turned-down middle seats of my SUV.

In Santa Rosa, she had no wrought-iron gate to guard,
No view through the wooden slats, and no back lawn,
Only a nicely manicured drought-resistant yard on a slight hill.
So she guarded three sides by running the perimeter
Wearing a new path not planned by the landscaper.

She no longer had a job or doggy friend, except lonely Marley
The Labradoodle next door, who occasionally
Poked his head between loose fence boards.
Uprooted and displaced
Porsche got sick.

After six weeks of only prescription dog food,
We fed her three parts affordable to one part triple-priced.
She had five years of good health, until
Nearly her seventh birthday in 2016.
Bloody cataracts appeared overnight.

Pannus, the vet said—an auto-immune deficiency.
Her body was attacking her eyes.
Expensive eye gel twice a day cleared the red film.
"Life-long diligence and consistency," the instructions warned,
"Can save your dog's eye sight."

Last year, so immobile we thought spinal injury, but her
Hospital stay revealed organs had begun to shut down—Addison's
    Disease.
Expensive monthly injections balanced her chemistry, along with
Prednisone wrapped in American cheese.
She regained her healthy early-senior years.

Two weeks after the Wine Country fires began,
Porsche suffered one night of too many trips outside
Until she no longer had the strength.
She walked out the back door one last time,
Sat on her patio pillow, ears erect.

First her right ear began to sag, her breathing labored—
Big belly breaths—not panting, as dogs do.
With chin on paws, she gently set the side of
Her too-heavy head on the concrete.
She was gone.

So fast, so unexpected.
What of the forty-five minutes left before her
Emergency appointment? Surely, the hospital could give her
More meds, special shots, different food.
Unprepared to lose her—no, No, NO!

Her beds and meds went to needy dogs, plus
Two tubs of foods, her toys, leash, and remedies.
Her favorite spot in the hall, where she could see
Bedrooms and front door, is bare.
No evil could have snuck into our house.

My welcome home greeting is silent.
Sticky spots once licked clean now dot the kitchen floor.
Five o'clock comes and goes—no nudging nose at dinnertime.
Empty space fills the place where her patio pillow padded her
Heavy bones—her perch to watch the birds and squirrels.

No more expense for medicine or heavy bags of food, no scheduling
Monthly injections; her hair no longer coats the carpet,
Collects in corners, or blows around the car.
No loud barking announces every delivery—it's quiet and empty.
My load is lighter, but my heart is heavy.

Jane Rinaldi

Writing a Poem

Whatever the subject, whatever the issue,
I revel in the rhythm of sounds,
for the repetition of a consonant,
a consonant cluster
that ricochets, vibrates,
reverberates on the ear.

Choosing a word
because of its musical energy
can move my thinking
unexpectedly
where I had no inkling
of ever wanting to be.

I delight
in unexpected syncopation;
it's like vocalizing
a Bob Fosse
gyration.

Sometimes, a certain occasional symmetry,
sure… (just for the fun of it!)
the resonance of rhyming vowels
can be pleasing to hear … to the ear.

But give me the unexpected,
the clandestine energy
of a motley medley
of a crew of consonants,
begging to be articulated!

El Diablo

In Central California
Hot air drags tumbleweeds
Catching both sand and dirt
Its swirling momentum inhales the earth

The wind lifts soil high into the air
Like the smoke of a genie escaping its lamp
It rotates and forms its own vortex
Becoming a new whirling dervish

I witness this birth of a Dust Devil
That heads to the highway I'm on
I see it is likely we'll meet
And collide in its chaos of harm

Navajos call them Chiindii,
Deceased tribal ghosts that are formed
From evil in lives left behind
And whose presence means illness or death

No way to escape I feel damned
As I head toward the twister in fear
The closer I come near I see its debris
Slamming the cars in front of me

Imagining the damage it's causing ahead
I pray it breaks loose and moves on
As I close in for impact it suddenly rises
And hops from the road to the median

Like an ice skater dancing, its willowy dust-arms
Extend to the sky in a rotating spin
But as it stretches and wobbles and withers apart
Its ephemeral life rapidly ends

Fingers of dust float up to the sky
As I quickly drive by
And whisper goodbye
"Adios El Diablo"

Life

I've been photographing everything
and everyone I love
with or without their knowledge or permission
forever.

My storage unit is packed with old photos
my digital chips and computers
have thousands of images on them.

What am I trying to hold on to
with all this photographing?
Life!
The lives of my children, family
lovers and friends
places I love
and even things I love—
my old truck being towed
away to the junkyard just last week.

Life—my own life—
such a fortunate woman I am
to have had/have this blessed life
and looking back at all these photos
only reinforces that.

Walking Home From the River

It was late in the afternoon
when I got down to the river today
but I took a nice cool swim anyway.

And as I walked the few short blocks home
again
I feasted on the fruits offered to me
by the bushes and trees along the way.

First there were the blackberries lining the path
leading up from our little semi-private beach
I go to almost every day
and then there were the dark purple plums
that come along right on the side of the road.
I felt so happy to discover them in the tall grass
when I bent down to retrieve someone's discarded trash.

And then, best of all, the tart green apples
just ripe enough to eat
that lay on the edge of my own dead end street.

Yummmmmmmm to all and much gratitude.

Best of all
it turned out I'd chosen the right path
at just the right time
to save a young garden snake
from being killed by a neighbor's cat—
she was just about to pounce on him
when I came along and shooed her away

Hurray!!

In My Sister's Garden

In my sister's garden
there are long-limbed dancers
trailing feathers and lace

twirling on lean emerald stalks
strung with berries
bright as Hessian garnets

in a waterfall of light
I swear I can see
unicorns supping on dew.

Margaret Rooney

Ragtime

A pulse beat, tip-tap
syncopated
prodigal encampment

of vagabond
flowers and
wild grasses
Canticles of color

arpeggios of sound
Blue trumpets
and green tympanies

Melodies
of bellflowers
and buttercups

A plainsong
of purple sage
and pearly everlasting

A carnal question
answered
in whorls
of sunlight

Skirls of birdsong
rumbas of thunder
and paradiddles
of rain

138   PHOENIX

Legions and legacies
of worlds unwritten
Unspooling
in ecstatic

beelines
humming harmonies
in a drunken
drowse
of honeyed light.

Polly and her Innocent Sisters

Time heals
so they say
And then, what
Do we feel less, or forgive more?

Time heals
so let's wait
for the mind to join the heart
and explain what defies explanation.

No, I don't want to be healed,
but perennially feel
the pain of the innocent
and the inescapable shame of being a man.

Quiet Music

Poems are the rough notation for the music we are
                                    —Rumi

Silence is the dash
between hot breaths

A shade that fades away
all pre-made perceptions

A safe interlude where truth
loosens the grasp of fault

That moment between arpeggios
Allows a space—a space to be

Before words after words
It is a phrase that matters

In the quiet within that quiet
Silence transforms to poem

Alicia Schooler-Hugg

Notes from Julia's Backyard

Evening shadows cross the lover's swing
Wood weathered now by life's patina
A breeze sends fallen leaves
To rest beneath the gargantuan fig tree
In Julia's backyard.

Chimes urged by random winds
Fill the space with music as sun abandons sky
The tree stretches its limbs
Toward a star-strewn canvass
Its leaves defined against the fading light
Of earth's ebb and flow in Julia's backyard.

We pause but cannot stop
Reach but cannot touch
Grow upward, outward, inward
Dancing life's pirouette
Pacing hearts
Until their beats are silenced
By the stillness
Of life's backyard.

Weightless bubbles
Borne by endless seas
Abandoned skyscrapers
Bear the weight of ages past
We grow new vines, keep time with time
Forge virgin pathways
Hide fears of endings
In life's backyard

As life's pulse quickens
We play at love
Step in time to its crazy rhyme
Bend its rules, hone its tools
Ignore tuition
Embrace fruition
Reach its sum
Then surrender to the truth
Of life's backyard

Eating Cherries

I am very careful how I eat cherries.
I pick through them, examine each one.
This one is wrinkled at the top, that one has a black spot, and
   here is a bit of mold.
The nice, round, plump, dark ones I put in my mouth,
bisect them in one sharp bite,
disembowel them with a flick of my tongue,
spit out the pit,
swallow the firm red flesh,
notice sweetness and crunchy texture.
my sister plunges her fist into the bowl, grabs a handful and stuffs
   it in her mouth,
stems, pits, black spots and mold.
Red juice drips from the corners of her mouth down her chin
   onto her blouse.
If she encounters a sour taste, she spits it all out, pouah!
Washes her mouth
and grabs another handful.

Twilight

In the tall grass behind the old chapel
Fluffy lambs play.

A black spider weaves a bright web
To catch the failing sunlight.

The Holy Virgin,
Blue robe faded and chipped,
Gazes sorrowfully,
Arms with missing hands outstretched
Towards the dead bird lying at her feet.

In the quiet evening,
The one red leaf on the maple tree detaches,
Begins its slow spiral cruise
Through the cooling air.
Strikes a head of grass,
Loosening seeds,
Slides halfway down the stalk,
Where it hangs suspended
As the land darkens.

39th Street, L.A., 1969

My door won't close—it flaps. Anyone can come inside.

Some say they want to help. The church ladies crawl in with
coffee hour cookies, the sour milk of human kindness from the
creamer, hauling the clothes of stiffs and street saints behind
them. I take only the dresses—drop waists, empire waists, shirt-
waists—the easiest to wear. I guess it's worth the Scripture they
make me hear. I fold the hems under my knees on the pallet so
the wheels I added won't lock up. When Social Services comes
calling, I'm a prisoner. They see the spice cake or the stick of real
butter and mutter *Must have a sugar daddy.* Write in their file
No food stamps. It maddens me so much I want to prove them
right —just one night again with a man that sweet. Last night
two brothers checked out the alley and brought another Frigidaire
box—called me the Queen of Cool—and made me a new front
room. Fixed up a hotplate to replace the Sterno can. At least these
Panthers are strong, even if the slogans they spout are too simple.

They don't ask what happened to my legs, but I can tell by the
way they don't stare there—they want to know. Fine. I lost them
back home years ago. But I won't say any more. Shins, calves,
heels, toes —they all walked backwards into my past—the only
thing that's real.

Jan Seagrave

Time Keeps Everything from Happening at Once

*—Attributed to Einstein, Feynman, Woody Allen
and to you, Charles*

I
Your watch alarm
sounds on the bureau
each morning at 8
No one can stop it
but you,
after you count to 20.

II
What were you thinking
hunched like Rodin's statue
on your side of the bed?
Was it about time?

III
You sang to me through a CD—
The Spider, a silly song—
your basso profundo
swirled down my ears,
and coaxed the trickster down the drain.

IV
All along you knew it was over.
You prepared me.
Even now as I rush to figure finances
you sing on the staff lines
of my spreadsheet.

V
We took half your ashes
in a boat to scatter in the Bay,
east of Angel
Island. Wind squeezed through the holes
in the old barracks, out over the waves.
Did you whistle?

VI
The breeze shifted.
White ashes aimed at the water
flecked a boat fender.
Don't fret, someone said,
It's just powdered Charles.

VII
Can I reconstitute you, like dry milk?
If I add water will you come alive
again as you did on the Bay
falling through the fathoms?

VIII
The only dirge I could sing was
My Bonnie Lies Over the Ocean.
Oh, Bonnie Prince Charlie,
the hero of Stuarts,
the Scottish Highlands,
oh bring back my Bonnie to me.

IX
A white paper heart
holds the rest
of your ashes.
You wait to go home
to the Strait of Georgia.
Then I can call you by your last name:
Seagrave.

X
Immobilized by Parkinson's
you still lie under the quilt
and call out for me.
Have you fallen again?
When I come to you
you are a mound of new laundry.
I hug the clean clothes to my face.

Wake-Up Call

Steven's voice is no different than when we were kids. He says, "Hey," when I pick up the phone and I tumble back, like a leaf in the wind. Seventeen and waiting for him to pick me up. Me and my girls, bored and car-less. We know he'll make the rounds through town eventually, in his ample-sized family vehicle, gathering bored friends from basement couches and awkward family dinners.

He'll find the three of us girls here in our lawn chairs, waiting for the sticky New Jersey heat to peel away so we can breathe. Waiting to go out, waiting to get high and talk and curl up all together like cats under the stars.

"Fifty?" I say to him now. "You're turning fifty?"

This makes me not far behind. This makes me frighteningly close to the middle of a very long life, or tipped towards the end of the time-span my parents were granted.

Fifty means I've known him for forty-eight years—at least, that's how the story goes. We met as toddlers, our mothers told us, while they drank their wine and told stories. Babies in the back of a PTA meeting. Or was it at the library? Steven wielded the power. An older, stronger child, he brandished a weapon, his toy statue of the Empire State Building. Fortunately, I was hard-headed, even then. I don't remember the event, and I hold no grudge.

We danced around each other for years in childhood, offering only subtle nods in the fierce social shark-tank of middle school, but plunked down together at the children's table at family dinners. Our parents laughed together, like drunken, happy hyenas. We watched from the side-lines, learning that the middle of life can be a time of deep amusement, if even in the face of occasional tragedy.

I loved to watch them laugh and listen to their banter, the theatrical retelling of stories, the literary references, quick witted puns, and occasional bursts into a Broadway tune. I drank it up: their mutual love of New York, each other's children, the lives they'd carved out for themselves, their friendship.

We sprung from these nests as artists, Steven and I—a painter and a writer. We chose opposite ends of the country for our abodes, and the demands of life and miles between us broke the continuity of our companionship. I no longer see him pulling around the corner, his cigarettes hidden in the glove compartment, sporting one bold earring and prepared with a joke for my father.

But still the phone rings. My friend is on the other end. He says "Hey." And I am home.

Unwanted Child

Beneath
the hardened heel
a ragged,
hungry
unwanted child
crawled

Unwanted child
belittled
bullied
battered
by the multitude

Unwanted child
hunted
cornered
trapped
like an animal
wild

Unwanted
child shackled
gagged
dragged
before a
corrupt court

Child
judged
unwanted
sentenced
imprisoned

Never again to see
the bright-blue heavens
or
the shimmering
green seas

Never again to see
the beautiful angels
that dance
in glittering
gowns

un-
wanted
naked child

Jo Ann Smith

Threadbare Heart

I do not know how many threads there were in the silk translucent
  sheets of my first love's bed;
      there were enough.

In that cathedral where we worshiped each other, one thread
  wrapped itself around my heart and
      I was changed forever.

We would change each other until changes led to
conflict, confusion, conditions and
      the thread broke.

The spool of my heart unwound leaving it threadbare and still;
  waiting for new love to
      compel it to race again.

Over time my heart will beat, bruise, bleed, break, even be brave,
  but in the end all that will matter is
      how high is its thread count.

Jo Ann Smith

To Gracie With Love

I did know I loved you when we first met;
I could not know then how much
I would come to love you.
But I knew I needed you
to be the radiant joy
that would refute the radiation
I feared the following day.

I saw in your eyes a longing
to know if you could love me too;
If I would take care of you;
if you would be safe with me.
I held your eight-week-old life in my hands
and promised your every need would be met;
you pledged the same to me.

It was quick and easy to fall in love with you:
you're smarter than a 5th grader,
you don't bark without reason,
you never chew what you shouldn't,
you always go potty outside.
Your reasons to love me are likewise uncomplicated:
food, shelter, health,
an occasional new toy,
a tempurpedic bed,
trust in my promise to "be right back."

Whether curled up like a croissant
or your long legs stretched out like a baby giraffe,
you are always elegant;
combining the essence of an old soul
with the lingering spirit of your youth.

When your eyes lock with mine,
yearning to connect,
you hold my gaze,
extend your paw to me
and confirm we're in the same pack.

We have grown old together, you and I
you at thirteen; that's my age, too.
Your black curly hair, like mine,
is spattered with curly gray.
Your growing discretion to come when called
parallels my penchant for more time on the couch.
My heart squeezes,
my breath gets shallow
when I imagine life without you.
I come home at the end of the day
to your wildly exuberant greeting
your helicopter tail spinning so fast
almost bouncing you up in the air;
that's how I know that neither can you,
imagine life without me.

I kiss your nose for the hundredth time,
tell you to get in your bed,
remind you you're luckier than people I know;
you accept this as a matter of fact.
I watch you circle in the bed you love
before settling on just the right spot,
then I hear the soft sounds of you going to sleep,
to dream about running with wolves.
but before I sleep to catch a dream too,
I think again, as I do every day,
how lucky I am to know you.

Liberty's Lament

(a rap)

Red, White and Blue

Mama, oh mama, what have we done?
Gone and elected a man with a gun
pointed straight at the head of all we hold dear,
automatic, loaded, clips of fear.

Mama I ask you, how can this be?
Whatever happened to solidarity?
A nation divided, citizens on edge,
healthcare, jobs, civil rights, the pledge

of allegiance to this dangerous fool
Mama, oh mama what shall we do?
When the time comes to act and not wait,
Mama, oh mama, will it be too late?

Huddled Masses

E pluribus unum lost in the mix
of hatred and bigotry, the promised quick fix.
Citizens blinded by the change that is here,
blanketed in layers of outrage and fear.

Many seeking a savior with an anvil-like hand
to pound down forces that threaten their brand.
Sixty-three million roiling in grief,
filled with disappointment, stunned disbelief.

Shouts from the right, hands wrung on the left,
streets filled with protesters angry, bereft.

Fear and uncertainty blanket the land,
truths held self-evident, will they stand?

Where does this leave this nation of ours,
fresh wounds to heal, leaving deep scars?
E pluribus unum, the port in the storm,
may that simple phrase be this country's norm.

From the many, one nation that's free,
forged by cries for true democracy.
E pluribus unum, sounds a clear call
to perfect this union before we fall.

Torched

Chaos descends on the land of the free
Covenant torn from mountain to sea.
First Amendment shredded, fake news the norm,
Blistered stories feed the viral storm.

Where once stood a Bill of Rights for all
now stands a crazed man with a maw.
Vitriol, venom, verbosity he spews,
signs executive orders that benefit few.

Impeachment, treason, hacked election, what more?
Will the courts of this nation reopen the doors
to liberty's promise and citizens' rights
to pursue life and happiness minus the strife?

Resist while you can, march, write and speak.
Push back the darkness, continue to seek
a pathway back to liberty's refrain,
"America the Beautiful..." will you rise again?

Fahime*

I found you displayed in a gallery.
Tossed forelock of paper shreds, a single strand askew.
Ears alert, black-brown water-color eyes watching
flared nostrils scenting, a slate gray muzzle
tapered softness.

Gray shades layers of white coat and paper-mache covered chest.
Arabic-lettered lines form mottled paragraphs
while gold and tan lightly curled strips of mane dangle against a
    long side.
A jeweled bridle and beaded turquoise halter evoke lineage
recall your ancient, royal heritage.

Dabs of gold enliven dark patches of canvas against your bright light.
A wide Egyptian blue ribbon highlights lettered swaths of hidden
    stories
revealed only to the native speaker.
Equine son of the desert
re-cognized in a framed portrait.

Heart-pierced re-collection of ancient memories
Samurai steed, my royal, wild Arabian.
Past-life resurrection streams tears
For the battle-slain loss
Your grace and dignity shattered by the enemy's thrust.

---

* Fahime is a Farsi word meaning intelligence or brilliance. This ekphrastic
  poem is inspired by a multi-media portrait of a horse. The artist works in
  paper-mache, acrylics, and print.

Home now, hanging on the living room wall,
The gallery reunion completed.
Our gazes meet knowing.
Serene and eternal, ethereal nuzzle
Once lost, forever found.

Deborah Taylor-French

Under the Storyteller's Hat

A hat is a giant ear kissing the top of a head. If the hat could talk,
  would it say?
  "All heads arrive hardwired at birth."
Out of kindness, it may add,
  "Cover your ears. Shield yourself from heads, *talking to
  themselves.*"
A profusion of tongues reeks from those walking towers of Babel.
The ear of the storyteller drinks in tales.
  Mostly lies.
Stories gush from not only the mouth—but also the eyes, the nose.
Other tales enter toes, freckles, and navels.
That's what keeps talking after death.
The dead become books the living forget to read.
Yet their fabrications live in us,
  unmoving tongues with quick minds,
  waiting for us to stop lying.
The living want fantasies, pretty pictures.
The departed no longer desire to be distracted
nor fall in love with ghosts.

Back to heads, telling story after story.
There's no stopping them.
Even if you walk away they spew jokes,
  shout opening hooks,
  whisper character arcs.
Holding evil intent, they trick us to losing our way in murder plots.
Memories unspool like bad movies.
  The worst tabloids kill original thought.
  Our childhoods awaken as winged horses
  as the wine dark sea roars at Pegasus.
When a storyteller opens her mouth,

oceans swarm out—
whales walk on water.
Bald Eagles swim the English Channel.
The octopi begin teaching Hellenic Greek
while flounders soar over Green House gases.
Given time—even ants will grow as tall as men,
wear tailored suits to tech jobs.
From on high, they mutter,
    "The segmented shall inherit the earth."
Ants in earphones jerk four legs in American Sign Language
    in praise of Sitting Bull.

As the storyteller nibbles peaches and honey,
the blind hat seethes snippets of tragedy,
adding to Homer's *Odyssey* in poor translation.
The lie of homecoming gushes from lion-headed spouts in Roma.
Even the water mutters,
    "Listen to me."
At times, it echoes in ten languages.
    "That other lion, *man*, he's not right in the head."
    Or "Surely, he's purely delusional."
At the end of days, all lions, living or dead,
demand the Nation of Venice return the four lions
stolen from Athens, Greece, issuing an ultimatum to
the United Kingdom to write a full apology and
demand the return of the Lord Elgin antiquities.

The storyteller's hat calls for a recess.
Yet one head continues speaking.
It claims to be the oldest.
Unlike the others, this head asks,
    "Why would a beautiful goddess keep a battered old man
    like Odysseus?"
Why do the gods do anything?
    For sport? A show of power? Spite?
    To tell the best story at the dinner table or between the

sheets?
To seduce mortals?
Remember, the gods have no shame.
Making fools of the living is the gods' eternal pleasure.
Ask Aphrodite, if you see her.
Stories love her, and her luscious hips.

Note: The title quotes a line from the *Braided Creek: A Conversation in Poetry,* a collection of poetic letters between Jim Harrison and former U.S. Poet Laureate Ted Kooser.

Sparks of Memory

I remember sparks of iridescent light from jellyfish
      under the water of Puget Sound
      off the deck of a ferry boat
Sparks of lightning hitting the horizon
      on a long car ride across Iowa
Fourth of July fireworks
      strictly supervised by my father
A New Year's Eve on a bluff in Puerto Rico

I remember a walk on the beach in Florida
      toward a red firestorm sky
      ashes floating in on high tide
      like black lace curtains in the sand

Sonoma and Napa sparks ignited compassion
      and gratitude, a contagious caring
      face to face, always asking, "Are you ok?"
Currents of love pervaded how we looked at each other
      as we walked up to the Cal-Fire men
      headed for their homes, thanking them
      for their courage and sacrifice

I remember witnessing the early days after the fires
      in Yellowstone and Mesa Verde Parks
      seeing the skeletal remains stripped
      of beauty and grandeur by a Nature that
      takes away but also restores life to us

I remember how ideas are born from sparks and
      ignite passions for change and hope

Waxing Moon

Caught in the diaphanous
light of the moon,
shadows hang in the air;
Listen, if you can,
for the sound of nothing,
then remember
what you hear.

Tommie Tin Ear

Tommie Peter LaBaron was a happy young lad.
No one in Laredo saw him angry or sad.
One night he took to drinkin' and fightin' with a knife.
He might have offended another man's wife.

Tommie awoke the next morning missing an ear.
He never did find that ear he held dear.
"This won't do," he said to himself aloud,
"I'll be hearing in circles and stand out in a crowd."

He picked up a tin can lying on the ground,
his pocket knife, sewing kit and a rock that he found.
He whittled and he hammered on that old tin can.
Then he stood back a very proud man.

Tommie sewed that tin ear to the side of his head.
No one seemed to notice and nothing was said.
But from that day to this, all you will hear
is what a good guy is Tommie Tin Ear.

Tommie Tin Ear was a cowboy by trade.
Forty and found was all he was paid.
A cowboy's night job is to settle the herd,
to keep them all quiet with a song or a word.

In better days Tommie could make the girls swoon,
quiet coyotes from howlin' at the moon.
The nightingales all sat high in the tree
listening to Tommie's concerts for free.

But when Tommie sang with that rusty tin ear,
the cattle all jumped up their eyes full of fear.
Soon they were running in a full-out stampede
no rivers nor mountains their way would impede.

When peace was restored, the cowboys did guess
what could have started that terrible mess.
If cattle got into some loco weed,
they should be shot, they all agreed.

Maybe a buffalo got sprayed by a skunk
or some geese with a cough or a wheeze as some thunk.
Then it was suggested it was an old Indian's ghost.
When they all voted, this got the most.

"No," cried the boss, "It definitely was not.
It was a wildcat with it's tail all tied in a knot."
No one was willing to argue with the boss lacking in sleep
not if their job they wanted to keep.

Soon it was discovered it was Tommie's tin ear.
That he couldn't sing, he just wouldn't hear.
They never could convince him that maybe it could
have been better had he made that ear out of wood.

They know they had to keep him from singin' to the cattle,
stay on the ground and out of the saddle
no matter what radical measure it took.
So they shot him in the leg and made him the cook.

Now if you ever find yourself in the Texas panhandle
and its Tommie Tin Ear you're wantin' to meet
just be sure you call by the right handle
'cause Tommie Tin Ear is now ... Peg Leg Pete

Nathaniel Robert Winters

Lakota Nation Weeps

Western train throws a loud whistle
bison won't be moved
car screeches to a whiplash halt

Buffalo hunters emerge
bringing down great beasts
too many to count
showing the endless tracks beyond

Locomotives belches black clouds
starts slowly, picks up speed
Whit way west

One hundred fifty years later
It is not tracks that scar Dakota land
but a pipe line
oil way south

Lakota nation weeps

Passage

We walked enchanted,
those rosy years,
Our skin was fresh,
Our hair was brown.
We walked beneath
The ancient trees
On ferny paths,
In dappled shade.

We rambled through the
Redwood groves,
Stole slits of sun
From shadowed paths,
Exulted spring's
Leaf-burst and bloom,
And crunched dried leaves
As winter neared.

We walked the paths,
We walked the years,
The trees gained girth,
Their shadows grew,
As we shrunk into
Smaller selves,
Our hair turned gray,
Our skin hung loose.

Now beneath
The ancient trees
Our steps are halting,
Our shoulders slack.

The trees endure
While we shall pass.
We walked the paths

Poems from
Sonoma County
Poet Laureates

The Poet Laureate is a Sonoma County resident whose poetry manifests a high degree of excellence, who has produced a critically acclaimed body of work, and who has demonstrated a commitment to the literary arts in Sonoma County. We honor here our poet laureates, recognizing that they have given so generously of their talent, their time, their love of poetry. Here are a few of their poems.

Terry Ehret 2004-2005
Geri Digiorno 2006-2007
Gwynn O'Gara 2010-2011
Bill Vartnaw 2012-2013
Katherine Hastings 2014-2015
Iris Jamahl Dunkle 2016-2017

Terry Ehret

Silence falls heavily on the ground
without breaking.
—Pierre Reverdy

Words have carried off the shore.

Where we stand, there is no easy
access. We pause at the edge
of the morning like explorers
who stumbled out of the wilderness
to stand above a gorge so wide
they could not have imagined,
and at its depths, a silver river threaded
by uncharted currents, pulled
by what could only be
a vast, unseen body. They knew
the journey was over:

no crossing possible.

Perhaps in the night when the fog
creeps up the valley from the sea,
words come teeming downslope from
our notebooks, from the shelves in the
library, from the tiny silicon
files in our computers, from the
backlogs of memories, from our
too-full dreams, come whirling
and rising down to the shore, flooding
the banks and carrying them away.

Now there are only depths—

our own, surely, but still unreachable.
Tiny fish swim there. Leaves
float on the surface in a kind of
slow parade. Sunlight glances and
echoes off the wooded cliff rising
on the opposite bank. All around
us the silence that has fallen through the night
without breaking.

Composed at Wellspring, on the banks of the Navarro,
Mendocino County, California

October Wind

The wind blows fierce and chill on Falcon Mountain.
The air is filled with leaves. Leaves
torn from willow, aspen, cottonwood,
more skeletal with each gust. They are losing
their light-catchers, their summer finery,
caught in flight, lit with their final days,
some vital radiance unseen until the moment
of letting go.
On the ridge overlooking Denver, stand
the fire-ruins of a grand house, now only
a noble jumble of burnt stone and chimneys.
Hikers sit among them, sheltering
from the wind, or reading the history
of Mr. Wealthy So-and-So whose money
raised the city his ruins overlook.
Far away to the west, our own hills lie smoldering.
A slow line of evacuees make their way back home,
if they're lucky, or sift through the debris for fragments
of what survived the storm. Acres of charred chimneys
like cemetery stones without names. Block after block
of rebar and ash. The hot days of October
with its toxic air, broken now and then
by a small, cruel gust.
Here, too, the leaves are falling, covering
the cinders, the scorched and thirsty earth.
Here we gather under the autumn sky, falling
together, bracing for the crash.

Terry Ehret

Poem for my Fifty-Seventh Year

This was the year I
fell into a crevasse, deep
in the glacial blue
of frozen love. The year I could not
sleep, and all the light
I knew collapsed like a star
weighted with darkness. The year
I stayed up all night
to chart the pulse of the hour,
to note the exact
morning the sun stood still on
its journey north and
waited there one beat, two beats,
three, then reversed its
way southward. This was the year
I lived half-in my
life, half-caught in ice. The year
the moon's shadow fell
across the sun, and in that
cold, remaining light,
some terror tore weeping from
its blind cage. This was
the year nothing could hold me.
From the four corners
of the room that was my world
came the terrible
dark horsemen. I couldn't step
outside for fear of
ambush, could not find a door
without tearing open
my heart. The year I had to

learn again to shed
wings and roots. To sit empty,
holding the stillness,
the terrible ache of nothing.

The Electric Company

The radio said it all
Sitting on the shelf above the sink
In the kitchen on 23rd and Noe

First thunder rolling across the sky
Then quiet
A necklace of lightning leaping out of
Recessed circle in the center of the radio
Streaking across the kitchen
The antenna crackling
The stench of burnt wire
Filling the room

Me sitting on the hard wooden chair
Pulling on my sneakers before school
All of us eating our oatmeal mush

The storm wailing outside
Banging doors and window screens
Rattling through the attic above our heads
Making every bone underneath our skin ache
The roots of each strand of hair on our heads
Alive with electricity

Having to wait
Outside for the old lemon school bus
To take us to school that day
Soaking wet by the time we got there

In Winter

I wear the dark blue socks
I gave you that first Christmas
Their crumpled shape pulled smooth
Against my icy feet

The straight-back wooden chair
Where you sat mending the spot
Rubbed thin your last well year
Your tailor hand moving up and up
In sure quick strokes

Morning light glinting off the needle
The long thread spiraling through the air
Disappearing in thick wool reappearing
Over and over
Leaving a fine red ridge across the heel

Lifting your legs into our beat-up Plymouth
Arrow our last trip to the hospital
You shouting out when I cut in front of a semi
On the freeway

What are you trying to do
Kill me

My Ancestors

Come to me
In the night
Their eyes
Looking out at me
Women in high-collared
Tight-waist dresses
And faces pinched
Like their lives

The polygamous wife
The raped stepdaughter
The blond child my mother
Holding her mother's hand

These women
Come to me
In my dreams
Wanting me
To see them

Gwynn O'Gara

The Promise

The pomegranate blossom falls from the robin's beak
as he presents it to his mate.
He plummets to the ground, retrieves the showy promise
and offers it again.
The angle of his golden beak suggests he will repeat this
as many times as he needs to.
She takes the wet flame in her mouth and begins to eat.
Thus, a vow is exchanged.
How often I drop the flower I want to give you.
Searching in the dust for my heart
I grow more constant.
Pollen, hope and song burn in my mouth
until you seize them.

Sea Cradles

Racing boats with sails of smoke
clog the channel. Soldiers patrol
the sand. *Ya viene el presidente!*
Children go on playing. How fragile
our coconuts. Between earthquakes,
land and sea stutter. We teeter, not
knowing how to fall. In this salt
soup she tore love's thorny flesh.
Silence pinned her, a bug on a tray
till she grew invisible wings.
Shells in her bed, kelp in her hair,
the backs of men pull her, all nerves.

Published originally in *Westview,* Spring-Summer 2015
Published previously in *Argestes,* Spring-Summer 2009

Gwynn O'Gara

The Drunken Mother

Dry lightning
  provokes the fire
     and it weaves up the mountain,
lunging at columbine,
    scorching corn lily
       and penstemon.
         Up slopes thick
           with grass and brush,
      flames crawl,
          devouring all.
      Wind drives the fire
         deep into the mountains.
           It destroys the oldest firs.
            Roaring to the top,
          the fire ravens the ridge to a crater.
               The wind dies.
             The fire stumbles,
         singes a hemlock,
       and drowns in snowmelt.

      Where a mighty pine lived,
   ashes flake in a pit.
    Where red fir fell and smoldered,
white lines stretch across blackened ground.

Yet the fire
  opened seeds
     that need fire   or bear
    to open.
  Kinnikinnick, bone white,
      comes back green.
        Undaunted,   lupine dances.

What is wind
but the uncontainable lover?
Flame and green are one.
Even the drunken mother loves.

Bill Vartnaw

River Road

for Chuck Torliatt

We are driving on River Road
Actually Chuck is driving
& I'm riding shotgun
In his cherried-out classic
I don't know what it is
I'm not into cars that way
but it's cool
& he's been working on it
Since he was in high school
& since I graduated this year
That's been at least two years
& he's got it just the way he wants it

We are driving on River Road
Above the Russian River
& between the redwoods
& Chuck says, "You want to see
My overdrive!"
& I say, "Yea!" because I know
He wants to show it to me
Though I don't know what it is
& Chuck steps on it
& we're going pretty fast
& then he pulls a lever
& our heads kick back
& I laugh
& he laughs!

& our parents are back at Armstrong Woods
Celebrating a birthday
Or an anniversary
& we're hanging out for the first time

Driving on River Road
I look down to see
The ferry boat that runs
From Rio Nido to Guerneville
Back & forth, back & forth
Maybe a half dozen times each day
A summer tradition that my family took each year
When I was a kid
That boat played Bobby Darin's "Splish Splash"
Over its loud speaker the first year
But then changed to Doris Day singing,
"Que sera, sera
Whatever will be, will be…"
Over & over & over again
Trying to create this idyllic moment
When you know the song came
From an Alfred Hitchcock movie
Where things weren't really as they seemed

You might expect
Dangerous rapids around the bend
Or that the river was polluted
& impossible to swim in without getting sick or dying
But this was California 1967…
The next day Chuck would put his car
"Up on blocks" & get ready
To report to basic training
In the fall I would go to college
Where I began to march against the war
I didn't see Chuck again
28 years later, I found his name
On the wall in Washington D. C.
I scratched it into one of my notebooks
Hoping one day I would write
This poem
Without anger
About driving on River Road

Because it was such a gift

My First Reading

Allen Ginsberg sitting on the floor
on stage at Freeborn Hall, 1970
playing a harmonium
& chanting Blake's Songs
        of Innocence & Experience

We sat on the floor & listened
someone started dancing
or he suggested it
& then we were all dancing
        no one sat

We started in a circle
holding hands
then we broke a part
"did our own thing"
came back together in smaller groups

We were dancing like hippies
at the Fillmore in '67
at a Sunday Zappa "Freak Out"
Frank hated it, flipped us off
thought us phony

Allen dug it
encouraged it, his recitation
more excited as the evening grew
This was my first poetry reading?
I went back the next night

Allen read his own work
he stood at the podium
the audience sat in seats, ponderous
3, 4 times as many as the night before
it was wonderful
        but no one danced

Pen to Paper

I touch pen to paper
a line—uninteresting
but miraculous

to the caveman cut off
by culture
I breathe the air here

& all the faded sounds
distant starlight
enters me in its relevant disguise

I've carried the croaking frog
from last week's walk
to dump it into this line

I couldn't find it in the landscape
but I can see it now
the ego is like that

as to the forgotten, the irrelevant, even the unknown
the ego washes its hands
& yet we claim an expanding universe

Katherine Hastings

What We Packed at 3 A.M.

The dog
the drugs

The cash
the cards

The elder neighbors who couldn't drive

We packed our fear
though it couldn't be contained

We crawled in our cars
as the fire raced

through its feast
of everything

of everyone
or everyone's dreams

Everywhere we looked
RED   RED

We called friends in the hills
No answer

We cried Jesus Christ!
No answer

The fire jumped and morphed
and ate some more

Garage doors wouldn't open
Trees blocked the roads

The red sky
grew wider and taller

and shot its off-springs
into the air

to ignite their own
smorgasbords

We unpacked our prayers
to all the gods

we don't believe in
And when we reached safety

we watched our phones
(we packed those, too)

for news and it
wasn't good.

Yes, we had each other.
Yes, we were alive.

But our world,
our beautiful Sonoma County world

What we packed
wasn't the mountains

wasn't the deer
the coyotes, the quail

wasn't the mountain lions
or mountain lakes

wasn't Willi's
or Fountaingrove

wasn't Coffey Park
or the field of larks

or the knowledge
it would take two weeks

to get back home
or that home would still

be there
or that the gorgeous golden grass

just outside our windows
would change overnight

into candles waving
their virgin wicks

Happiness

after the fires

We'll find it again

Perhaps not as much
as the dog in Scotland
who wagged his tail so hard

so often
it had to be
amputated

Not that happy.
But
Okay happy.

After two years in a pound
he found a home.
It will take at least that long

for some in Sonoma County
and when they do
we'll wag our behinds

like Buster
though I don't care what they say
there's no such thing

as a *forever home.*

Note: Buster, named "the happiest dog in Scotland" is a Staffordshire
Bull Terrier who had to have his tail amputated due to excessive wagging.
Reported in the San Francisco Chronicle on November 13, 2017

Fire Weather on Wagnon Rd.

The horse that galloped over the dry field
kicked up enough dust to leave our throats dry.
Heat shimmers in air. Air heavy with smoke
That's from someone else's fire. Even
The birds are seeking refuge in their own
shadows. Feels like rain, but it can't, too much
pressing down from the sky. A spade, the dust,
the inheritance of something wild: the horse
Silk and muscle, cuts and runs far out—
We'll never catch her. We'll always try.

Iris Jamahl Dunkle

After the Seventh Night of the Northern California Wildfires

For seven nights there were no stars, only sky
muted by smoke. On the first night, the dry bones
of the past rattled the eaves of valley oaks
on the hillside. Then, raging, hot-throated wind stirred
and sparked flames. Until the mountain
cracked open: red-lava heart pouring down.
A man or a woman is most alone
when he or she looks at the moon stained red,
at the hillside glowing hot as a stoked furnace.
Every house feels to be a single cell
of the same beast: fragile and ignitable.
And the days drift on—safety looming off
horizon, a far-off ship. But so long
as we can see far enough we never tire.

Iris Jamahl Dunkle

Wild Horses

The song keeps visiting me like a ghost.
I never liked it. You never liked it.
But there it is just the same floating
like a satellite in my grief torn mind.
Last night the dog tore out of the house, barking.
He must have smelled something wild.
I followed him outside to the porch where stars
pressed me down, closed the door.
Sound ricocheted off the dark hillside.
A cloud of hoofbeats cluttered the dark air
as if a pack of wild horses was rushing at me—
I could feel their muscles tightening.

The way the mustang pony
you bought when I was seven,
tensed and showed the white fear of its teeth
before it struck out, before you taught me
to hold tight and ride even what is most untamable—
Under the powdery stars,
the forest shuddered. The dog barked.
And the sound galloped away so fast
I could feel the weight of you lifting.

Still with us in Spirit

What stands out in thinking about our three deceased poet laureates is their commitment to poetry and the word and their generosity in mentoring young and older poets in Sonoma County and beyond.

The county's first poet laureate, **Don Emblen, 1999-2001**, made it his mission to display locally written poems on public-transit buses, a mission Bill Vartnaw carried on later in his plans to install bronze plaques to display poems in public spots around the county. Don Emblen was a major force at Santa Rosa Junior College, inspiring generations of students with his love of honest, observant composition, and sharing poems written for colleagues almost daily.

David Bromige, 2002-3, a mentor to hundreds of young poets and known for his generous spirit and impeccable syntax, was involved in the Bay Area poetry movement early on, with his work with Robert Duncan and Robert Creeley, and he transferred his influence to many here in Sonoma County.

Mike Tuggle, 2008-9, with his evolving family and poetry style, featured Cazadero's natural isolated beauty, the local animal life (he was a goat farmer) and how its recent arrivals adapted their lives to be in harmony with our ancient hills. He was well known for organizing poetry readings and workshops as well as working with Poets in the Schools, a favorite activity of many of our laureates.

While these few words cannot convey the scope of the talents and activities of these three poet laureates, we can at least see their clear commitment to mentoring and celebrating the written and spoken word. Here is a poem by Don Emblen which appeared as part of his obituary.

Don Emblen

Forgetting and Remembering

When someone close to you just goes and dies
despite your prayers and urgencies of will—
a son or daughter, say, or aging parent,
aunt or uncle, neighbor, a long-lived dog
whose soft, sprawled form before the fire had long
become a reassuring hump in the floor plan
of your house of days, we feel betrayed—
again. Lost memories of that first harsh dying,
when the womb's warm promises were torn away,
now carry us off on bitter floods.
We flounder in the black, cry out
for light and buoyancy through leaden nights,
forgetting that we are but fishes
rising to some dimly understood surface
for our modicum of vital, lethal air.
No one promised immortality,
no one but in grief forgets that life
as surely throbs in the close embrace
of dark waters as in the daylight fountain singing,
bright as blood.

... and then

Fire draws eyes, mind, ears
into its promiscuous path.
Thought sucked into ash
leaves charred mind
smoldering at the black river's edge,
the fire-licked mind dying the death
of self-consumed blaze,
falling first to ember
then to ash,
which is not dead, you say,
but only changed.

—Fran Claggett-Holland

When Random Sharks Attack

When a frenzy of orange threshers
battle-sharpened yellow teeth ablaze
rushes to take your home
nothing can prepare you for the carnage
Denial an oh so temporary refuge
briefly houses your future plans and hopes
It too is overtaken by voracious marauders
I speak as one consumed
I dream of a huge red bear
I am empty sad feel worthless
I don't know what to do be still or fight
Luck had saved me up till the present
I'm watching scores of rock doves swoop
these Oakland hills evade the stoop of circling
red-tail hawks eye level with our refuge from
the fire oh that black senses-deadened early morning
blind eyed rush without a single dorsal fin
to warn or woo while now and here in hills
across the Bay awake to strangeness:
curse of phantom pain we know but still
we want the easy comfort of our house
the sense of going home to what we know
to what we together purchased once we married
I seek a new thesaurus to explain things
Here in space where furniture doesn't fit me
in and out of my body feeling freaky
If it's true that attachment equaled suffering
I've been shoved on to the road of enlightenment
all too quickly here in a region known as Purgatory
atoning for my sin of routine comfort

We almost died
We did not die
We lost a house
And all possessions
Much more remains
In the rubble of our pain
The innocence of sharks
very much maligned

Ed Coletti

Ashes Among the Remains

My father responded

Just throw them away

I did not nor did I cast them into
ocean or bay where we'd fished
flounder and fluke nor strew them
over the golf courses where he'd hit
multistage rockets rising from half an inch
then to a foot above fairways
to summarily explode
hundreds of yards into the future
other worldly fireworks released
by his elegantly compact fury.

Instead I left them in their box
a golden shiny tin ossuary
next to my mother's on the top shelf
of my bedroom closet
where I did not have to make decisions
and I incidentally could visit them daily
until our house burned down
in the California wildfires
October Ninth 2017

I don't intend here to dwell upon
the nightmare that fire is
I will not detail the feelings we had
as we evacuated in one of our cars
along with the family terrier and nothing else
though later we did contemplate

Dad's and Mom's remains further
consumed by 1500 degree flames
extending their years-earlier incineration
in an oven at the crematorium near Petaluma.

Were it not that my parents lived well into
their nineties I so sick depressed and barely 74
might feel prepared to let go of the tangible rim
to the bottomless jar of all that remains
to the what or the where or the not.

The Spiral Stairway

The spiral stairway
went nowhere,
though it once went
from ground floor to
second floor before
the wild fires that
taught them what
wild really felt like,
what fire really looked like,
when they evacuated
in the night, managed to
take only their cat,
her computer
and their car which took them
beyond the flames in the
forest bright
brought them to safety and the
memory of that spiral stairway
that conveyed them up and down
for decades with cat, with
computer and the sounds of the
forest now stilled by the fury
of the fire.

Falling

In these awe-filled days of fire and flood
We watch and wait and wonder
When that fierce hand
Might reach at last for us.

Those of us not yet touched by calamity
Quake, knowing in our bones
That though we may be spared
This time, time will level us all.

No magic amulets, no prayers,
Good deeds or good looks
Can promise protection
From our terminal condition.

And those who have watched a child
Swept forever from our arms
Or fled the flames that swallowed
Our hopes and our memories

Or hid from the bombs
Or the predator's gaze
Know that nothing now will ever be the same—
As if anything ever were.

For all of us are falling
Like ashes, like rain,
Like petals or leaves;
But we all are falling together.

And if we knew, in truth,
There was nowhere to land,
Tell me: could we know the difference
Between falling and flying?

I Meant to Write

I meant to write in my poetry journal today and yet somehow it feels wrong, as if it's too private a response to a shared disaster.

Nothing happened to me. House is fine. Kids are bored but good. Husband is back to work. Even the cat has settled down. On the surface, nothing immediate has changed.

Yet everything has changed.

I take the dog for a walk down the alleys in my neighborhood and every pile of leaves that was wholly innocuous two weeks ago seems like a threat today.
Did we always have so much dry debris? We must have but somehow I didn't see it. Or I saw it and failed to recognize the power smoldering inside it.

Two weeks ago I woke up and all that mattered to me were my kids, my animals and my spouse. Stuff be damned! And now I find myself gleefully shopping—that new sweater is a sign the fire is over, done with. Every little thing I accumulate is spurious proof that we do indeed have dominion over the earth. Isn't it?

Now is the time to support the local community—buy the wine, eat out, get a haircut. These are the things I did before the fire—without thinking, as a matter of course.
But yesterday I found myself in the hairdresser's chair and the silent thought bubble over my head was: Take it all off.

Take it all off. There has to be some physical sign. Some small stupid sacrifice. Hair to burn so I can pretend to the gods I really took part in this tragedy.

I finally got up the nerve to watch the harrowing video clip made by Berkeley Engine 16 as they drove into town early Monday morning to fight what they assumed was a "large grass fire." Originally, the five engines from the SF area were to regroup at the Kmart parking lot but, when they got close, they realized the building was already engulfed in flames. So they drove around "looking for something to save."

"Looking for something to save"—I can't get over that phrase. Don't you want to scream: SAVE F—ING EVERYTHING! All those stupid do-dad things we touch a thousand times, all the while infusing them with meaning. Some FB asked people what was the silliest thing they grabbed on their way out. People took cat trees and false teeth and baby books. Obviously valuable things and completely random things that happened to be right by the door.

Berkeley Engine 16 did find something to save. They saved the whole side of one Santa Rosa street. After the fires had died down somewhat, the guy making the clip remarked on the fact that one side of the street had completely burned down while the other side remained "relatively untouched."
He called it "the line of sorrow."

That "line of sorrow" will be the new prime meridian for a lot of people in Sonoma County. It will be the line dividing the time before from the time after—the time when you had a house and mementos, socks and shampoo and scissors (if you could find them) from the time when you had nothing—nothing but kindness of strangers. It was the time before you knew you had that and had it in spades.

I, too, am "relatively untouched" by the fire—except for the new hairline that now breaks at my jaw instead of my shoulders. Six inches less to singe.

Judy Anderson

Backdraft

you bear down on me, all heat and sweat
each acrid breath more shallow than the last
I am tinder

I imagine hooves of fleeing deer
ash-laden birds falling
And I swear I can hear the trees cracking

shovels against flame, your body against mine
soft flesh engulfed
what rises from this smoke?

fire—our backdrop, our foreground, our foreclosure
the last patch of sky surrendering to gray
even the sun yields to this burn

I am the fleeing deer, the falling birds
my wings beat against your futility
no suppression, no containment

I am lost in your backdraft

Los Incendios

Dia de los Muertos came early this year,
fueled by howling Diablo winds.
Burning altars, Santa Rosa razed
sallow ashes mark migrant-picked vineyards
where work fed familia.

Dancing skeleton's soot-covered grin
wiped away by the remains of furious explosions
claiming once-breathing
now ancestors,
su recuerdos uncollectable.

This year the abuelas' celebration tables
fill with prayers to the Virgen de Guadalupe,
entreaties to honor the grief-stunned ones
not lost to the ancient ritual
encircling their lives.

Locate Belief

Where were you when Dante's Inferno leapt off the page
a myth unhinged? Stricken-horror, terror trapped
circles of loss, consumption complete.

Suffering souls gladly the host of hell crackled
torment, taunted laughter, devoured life,
rain of smoke and fire fueled by foul winds.

Where were you when Shiva's dance of
destruction consorted with Buddha
to awaken impermanence?

Life reincarnate, the promise of Brahma's rise
Gautama's everything from something leaves nothing,
dangling discomfort.

Where were you when mother earth lost her balance,
elements switch-tripped explosion screaming
can you hear me?

Where are you now?

Jeffrey Goldman

Fire in the Wind

The wind catcher moves
From something unseen
No sound from the tubes
Like magic it seems

Nothing else is moving
Including redwood trees
A little breath of wind
Only seen by me

Interesting this wind
That you cannot see
Unless it carries death along
With a tide of uncertainty

Howling like its angry
A rampage soon to be
Wind that cools and cleans
Becomes a sea of misery

Unforgiving and heartless
Hero's stand and retreat
Destroying all in its path
Death in the driver's seat

After a while the winds calm down
Its anger seems to subside
While we wait for the wind that cleans
To blow the smoke aside

Then we mourn and rebuild
And wait for the wind that cools
Because that's why we all live here
Sonoma coast breezes really rule

The First Fire

We sway with the flames
Hand shadows on the cave wall
Slap them to the rock and
hold them fast, fast

Spit red ochre around fingers
knuckled and gnarled
red like blood of the four-foot
whose entrails entered ours

Hand prints
like treetops in fall
logs of a sparking fire
mouths that spray words

Stone is cold on our bones
Dreams remain even
when the eye of the cave
opens to the sun

October 10, 2017

Sonoma, Napa, Solano, Santa Rosa
will never be the same.
Las Vegas concert goers will never be the same.
Hurricane victims will never be the same.
This City, That City … the list too long.

New perspectives.
New fears.
New ways of thinking.

Frustrated with nature.
Angry with wrong-doers.
Angry with bureaucracy.
Angry in general.

We now know the unimaginable can happen.
We now know there are no guarantees.
We now know what we don't want to know.

What will we take away?
What have we learned?
What do we need?

We need time to process.

Our beautiful Northern California landscape,
disfigured by ash and rubble,
looks like a war was fought
in its yards and parks and on its hillsides.

The unthinkable happened.
How can so many people lose so much?
Tears spill down weary cheeks.
We carry on, adjusting to a new normal.
Trying to make sense of that
which cannot be understood.

There is the before.
And now—the after

The camaraderie and sense of community,
the goodness of people.

My writing partner asks if I am okay.
I answer, "No, but I will be."

A Rage of Wildfires

Fires glared and swirled and spat hot flame
And dared the squads who fought them
Fueled by winds they could not tame
Until Mother Nature caught them

Our roads display their insane wakes
And pale retardant dust
Clings to their sides like green iced cakes
A monstrous oozing crust

Lives were lost and heroes found
Survivors still have needs
Signs of gratitude abound
For first responders' deeds

Today I wept as I passed by
A graveyard of charred homes
Children's bent swings caught my eye
And twisted auto bones

A rage of wildfires caught our town
Consuming all within their paths
It took a while to calm them down
To satiate their glutton wraths

Alone in Hell

Smoke.
Frightened.
Need to find family.
Heat all around.
Paws burning.
Hide.
Jump down in hole.
Hear the monster roaring.
Can't stop shaking.
Want my family.
All alone.
Smoke found me.
Coughing.
Darkness.
Hurting.
Where's my family?
Tired.
Can't cry anymore.

They Are Us

Fierce and unrelenting,
The wind blew toward us.
Charred paper, shards of lives
rained down in our yard,
ten miles from the fire. Ten miles away!
Is the ash of people, animals,
raining down, too?
Are we breathing each other in?

On Wednesday, two days after
the fire tore through,
a friend saw a man flick
his cigarette from a car.
She wanted to chase him down,
rip open his door, holler
"What are you thinking?"

Living here, the suffering is close;
We are shredded by loss.
Now we know firsthand: no
California dry season will
ever seem benign.
The ash of people and animals
floated down, too.
They are us. We breathed each other in.

Annita Clark-Weaver

October Storm

My heart is heavy; overcast with grief
Skies darken, sun grows pale and weak
Distant rumbling—echoes of the past.
Alone, strange voices fill my ears.

My throat tightens; I cannot move.
The winds pick up—I swirl and bend
The heavens crack—my world splits wide
Releasing pouring tears.

Rebecca del Rio

When I Thought My House Would Burn

When I thought
It would burn, my house
Would certainly join the
Fire, become fuel
Like so many others
I imagined those papers
Settled in deep boxes
Slumbering in a storm
And I was grateful
I'd have no chore to undertake,
No decisions to make.

I imagined the roof, flat
And sieve-like allowing
Fire, like winter rains, to pour
In and mercifully
Choose what goes, what
If anything, stays.

I imagined books, photos,
Paintings surrounded and
Surrendered to the insatiable
Appetite of destruction, so like
My appetite for acquisition
That leaves little to imagine,
To fill with emptiness.

Two years ago, I sifted
Through years
Of greeting cards Rich
Could not part with until

He parted with his life
And left behind treasure
Of no meaning to others.

Returning home, I saw
My own small history,
Quietly cluttering corners
Swallowing the present.
Like fire, I swept through
Drawers and cupboards,
Clearing away the moments,
The mementos of times
Lived and asking remembrance.

When I thought my house
Had burned, was burning
As I climbed out of Paro's
Narrow valley towards Tiger's Nest
I carried, not birthday cards,
Not books or grandmother's
quilts and paintings,
But the rabbits and squirrels,
The pumas and skunks, deer
And trees, tucked in my heart.
I knew then what I loved.
I know now what I will
Carry when, like others
Before me, I flee this life
For the unknown, fires
Of living fading behind me.

Joanell Serra

Smoke in My Eyes.

The smoke hits me when I wake.
For an instant, not more, the scent stirs a bubble of anticipation.
Years of conditioning has made my brain a trickster.
This could be the scent of a campfire, drifting back from childhood.
The scent of star-filled summer nights,
Of afternoons reading by the fireplace,
Of evenings sitting by a fire-pit in Carmel,
sipping red wine while a bag-piper salutes the sunset.
The scent of love.
Instead the new reality sinks in.
This smoke is different.
This smoke means the wild fires continue to rage just north of us,
That our Sonoma haven is not safe tonight,
That our friends and neighbors struggle, displaced or worse.
That the lush green hills where we hike are blackened.
That the wineries where we taste wine and visit with the wine-makers are devastated.
That the landscape of our lives is being slowly eaten away by this engulfing, raging monster.
That the strange looking orange orb in the sky is the sun, hidden in smoke.
That we live now for the word *containment.*
That many lives have been lost.
This is not the smell of camp songs, marshmallows sticky in our children's hair, Christmas Eve magic, Bing Crosby's crooning, binding friendships or winter romance.
This is the smell of chaos. Of smoky black vineyards, houses turned to dust, destroyed schools, charred churches, and the bones of the families who did not escape.
This is the smell of our communities hurting, lives devoured, and our history burning.
This is the smell of loss.

Clare Morris

The Silence of Ash

Evidence of what was …
cleansed of identity
burned into future
unknown

Carried on wind's perfidy
that does not ask
Where have you been?
In whose body?
How long?
No questions

No hint of new destiny
No why ash falls on stone
river
root
clod of seeded soil

Ash eternally dies into birth
a pattern that comes
from the stars

Clare Morris

Air that Burns

Fire and dry wind
ravenous tongues
claim their catch

Fierce ecstasy
smoke strangle
black blizzard
death dance

Ash flakes that were
that were
were

Gates and Chimneys

It's a tragedy when people are wiped out
killed in an accident far from home
knocked down by crime or illness
leaving behind a life's collection of
things

Heirs sift through stuff
furniture, papers, clothing
smell years of mildewed milestones
decide what to keep and what to
lose

It's different when the stuff is gone
taken by fire, and people who survive have
only gates and chimneys
from a lifetime of
memories

Victims stand in charred emptiness
remember furniture, papers, clothing
smelling only soot and ash
wonder how to get beyond the
loss

To Go On

to go on as rain
overdue, patters ash
driveways lead
nowhere
flames fizzle
fire trucks follow
lonesome roads
home

to go on as chimneys
naked, stand alone
rubber duckies ooze
on burned-out cars
twisted wheels whir
reporters pack up
looking for the next
big story

to go on as evacuees
haunted, remember
fists pounding
flames engulfing
animals shrieking
houses exploding
pages, charred, floating
through noxious air

to go on as husbands
long for wives, children
mourn parents, sisters
console brothers, babes

cry for elders, families
in thousands
reel, no longer
whole

to go on as survivors
dazed, open wallets, search
closets, buy food
for the ravaged,
neighbors hug neighbors
grateful for what was
what is lost forever
what remains

Equus Heart

Within the cleft
the memory
of fleeing
forewarns

rising upward
shudder of fear
seizes upon
the scent of death

my unbridled face
shoulders riveted
flanks pressed
electric peril

pace of strength
against the wood
cladded confines
attest the force

run to the hills
break the rails
atomic steel
away now—away!

the furied night
the aching breath
the furnace vortex
ascent the truth of fear

going going going
away must away
blind ever the path
from the burning barn

crushing death dust
ashes profusion
ghostly strobes
lights on the road?

approach the slow hands
anoint the trembling withers
and quivery hell-singed mane
calm this equus heart

Pamela Fender

Colors of Fire

Red flames of fire
Firefighters in yellow
Black hills
Gray ashes
Smoky air
Lungs hurt, eyes burn
Brand new cemetery
aptly named Journey's End

Louise Hofmeister

Dispatches from the Fire Zone

When daylight shows the aftermath
of fire-eaten bones and ash
from somewhere deep a primal sound:
Ashes, ashes all fall down

All around the Mayberry Bush
The winery's gone, the grapes were spared.
We grabbed the passports
Forgot the albums unaware

We stare at mystery
what was lost
what remained
more arbitrary than ordained

And everywhere the t-shirts shout
Sonoma Strong
Sonoma Strong
Love lingers when the smoke is gone.

Stephanie Moore

Fire Ghosts

Morning mists rising
in white puffs between hills
look like smoke;
from my deck, I inhale
cool, damp air, yet
sense something acrid.

Orange light to the west
at sunset could be fire;
winds that charm golden leaves
to dance can carry embers
to vineyards and rooftops,
sparking conflagration.

How long will it be before
I see the leaves of lemon trees
on my patio, the white oleander
flowers, without thinking they
could catch fire, curl, burn?

How long before I look
at photographs on my roll-top desk
without seeing faces devoured
in gray disintegration,
or hear a helicopter overhead
without thinking fire, fire?

My home was surrounded
on three sides by six wildfires;
over nine days, I received
five urgent alerts;

I had time from sixty miles away
to visualize the fire's progress,
room to room, consuming
furniture, keepsakes, roof and walls.

Yet here I am, home again,
with everything intact;
with full-hearted gratitude
I wonder how long before
the ping of a text won't
startle me to vigilance,
to hear again that mechanical,
disembodied, dispassionate voice
warning me that fire
is rapidly approaching, get out,
get out; I hear it upon waking.

I know how very fortunate I am.
I hope that voice stops soon.

Red Necklace

I returned home to Sonoma
after firestorms
to discover a gift from my sister
on my front doorstep.

A necklace,
its charm a deep red heart
set in onyx crystal,
glowing powerful scarlet,
tiny points of light sparkling hard
like diamonds.

The jewelry artist herself
a survivor of fire; in the
Smoky Mountains, she, too,
had faced a derecho of flames:
lives, homes, livelihoods
lost in wind-driven inferno,
a thousand natural shocks
sent to all in its path.

She designed the necklace from
dichroic glass, forged in fire
at fifteen-hundred degrees,
molten crystal and kiln-fused glaze
cooled to iridescent beauty,
opalescent, fire contained within.

I wear the necklace
as a pact between survivors,
as a gift given in loving kinship,
a beautiful circle emerging from fire,
a blessing lifted from ashes,
I wear it as a prayer.

Jo Ann Smith

Rise up

This wasn't a marshmallow fire;
no campfire delight or child's play.
No one called it beautiful
or mesmerizing.
No one cuddled before it for warmth.
No one stared into its flame
to watch the color
mysteriously born in fire
or look for imaginary shapes of
people, animals, places or things.
The images from this fire were real—
people, animals, places and things.

This was a fast, fierce, forceful, fire;
angry, raging, deadly, indiscriminate;
whipped by a frenzied Diablo wind,
released from the Inferno,
devouring, possessing, polluting;
leaving nothing but ash and soul.

Phoenix has not risen yet,
still blinded by ochre smoke
turned into black air,
obliterating the sun
to which she is drawn;
but she is perched
on her pyre
to resurrect again
renewed, resolved,
awaiting the dawn.

Becoming Disconnected

Sonoma/Napa Counties October 2017 fire

There are rules … punctuation and grammar
For creating cohesive sentences
For connecting characters in a story
For describing complex ideas
And ensuring they make sense
But there are no rules to follow
To reconnect my life
To the path it once took

The massive fire
Came too close
It filled the air I breathed
With the substance of burnt lives
My chest ached
With the pain the air carried
It was acid in my throat
And prickled the tissues in my nose

When the fire was extinguished
Burnt pain no longer filled
The air I breathe
Nor bathed my mind in tears
But the fire remained
A punctuation point
It had defined my path and damaged it

Now I cannot find
The dropped stitches of my knitting
So that I can weave them back into my whole
For now I will mourn my loss
A little while longer

Hell Comes to the Valley

I see the flames
Roaring red
and yellow
and grey
Consuming forest
jumping fences
igniting
acre after acre
Edging closer—
ever closer
striking at pine trees
blackening grass
Smoke fills the lungs
of the bipeds
of the quadrupeds
and all that slither
in its pathway
It singes the feathers
of birds caught in flight
devours all screams
Life is trapped
in terror
in a killer's dream
The road is closed
to freedom

Survivor's Guilt

Ten days after the fires began,
I unload my car of
Clothes, mementos, supplies.

My evacuated guests have returned
to their homes,
Leaving behind an aura of stillness.

The lock on my fear unhinges.
A foul wind of memories
Bellows from a dragon's jaw.

Hysteria etched on a friend's voice,
Expressions of fear her mantra;

Cinders wind-blown for three miles,
Fallen a foot from my garage;

The flimsy feel of a garden hose,
Handed to a roof-bound neighbor.

Ten days after the fires began,
I think of the bodies consumed by flames,
Their ashes now resting in my lungs.

Hoarse sobs scorch my throat,
As I kneel on my unsinged rug.

It's Not Ash

"My car has dandruff."

"Yes, that's it exactly."

"This cloud of tiny white flakes
that dance upward when I open the door,
these flecks that settle on my sleeves
and waft toward my face,
peppering the lawn
and the driveway
and the road."

"My car needs a good shampooing."

"Maybe if I drive fast enough
it will all blow away."

The First Blue Sky

It's blue
real blue, not tainted
not tinged with smoke
not ugly on the edges and only normal if you look straight up

It's all blue, in all directions
and there are no clouds

This is the most beautiful sky I've ever seen

It's almost as lovely as the shade of blue
on the fleet of PG&E trucks
all carrying new telephone poles
that I passed on the way to work this morning

Reading the Press Democrat

You're on the way to Reno   say,
a passenger with her daughter to
get away   or maybe,   one
of many,   commuters
driving down I-80.   It's another
bad air day   more evacuations
Nixle alerts   but worse
you notice
the sad eyes of a woman you
recognize   once worked with, side
by side.   Her photo in The North
Coast section. Her son's mentioned,
eighteen months   and loss of
home to the Tubbs Fire.   There,
she stands amidst the rubble &
char, shoulders slumped
in maroon knit top   the gaze
distant.

As distant as the stretch
of sepia haze over flocks
of ducks plovers   the double-semi
hauling garlic   turning off
the Truxel Road exit   as you pass,
and you might realize then,   there will be
no getting away.

You fold the paper,
gaze out upon the smoke,
the Central Valley canopied.   Last
you knew she was on maternity

leave. Everything's
flipped   cars   trees   tossed
like leaves.
People.   She
used to be the one counseling
those in need   the one
in charge   say,
keeping office.

Christine Berardo

Phoenix
(a haiku)

Ash in place of home
Photos gone, relics of youth:
All is forgiven.

Roger Lubeck

Smoke and Ash

Smoke and ash
confusion and chaos
flee barefoot
in the night

Smoke and ash
packed but not ready
north or south
nowhere is safe

Smoke and ash
sorrow and grief
drowns out hope
no phoenix rising.

Barbara Hirschfeld

A Piece of Paper

A piece of paper
Drifted down
From the sky
Amidst the ash and dirt
The paper was part of a dictionary
It landed by the sanctuary door
The words
Tempest
and
Temple.
And so it was
From the tempest to the temple
From the storm of fire to the sanctuary
And on the edge of the page
Partially charred
The word
Temporary...

"Take your valuables," they say.
They are scattered

Scattered over rooms and fields
The pieces of my life
Are not to be gathered
Cannot be gathered

Can all of what I care about
Fit on this memory stick?

Drifts

"… the title of this life chapter is *The Incredible Lightness of Being.*" Arthur Dawson, whose home was lost in the 2017 Sonoma County fires.

The day camp kindergartener drifts to my side
and stays there. He wants to transcribe
my words into his secret baby language,
which he can write both in "regular" letters
and Chinese-like characters.
He tells me of the time, years ago,
when he lived in outer space,
gathering his mother's secret baby words.
Now, on this planet, he has lost both home and school.

I am breathing in others' histories,
their floating libraries,
wandering recipes,
porch mornings,
piano and pillows.
This gray confetti, adrift
on this leveling wind,
visits my heavy lungs.

The scatter of my thoughts, the scattered ash of these pasts,
it is said we will know again the lightness of snow.

Fire Dragon

I didn't see its fangs but
I smelled its breath
I didn't feel its heat but
saw its rufous belly, red wings,
and the ravens cloud of its thoughts.
Its claws ripped me but not
through my own flesh.
Rather through a mycelial network,
through the interdependent root
system in these twin valleys.
Through the spasm I feel when
another's tree house is yanked out.

The beast has folded its wings,
withdrawn its claws. Graven image,
black, red, voracious, do not leave me.
Stay singed in my consciousness.
I need to know you, know you
are ready to spring again.
Know safety as illusion.

The Waning Moon

is still orange
late on this early October night.
The air is still filled
with the acrid smell
of smoke
from smoldering trees
and vines and pastures
and people's burning homes
filled with all their necessities
treasures and
irreplaceable memories.

So much loss
so much pain
it will be a long time
before much will be
restored again.

Though some, of course
can never be.

After the Firestorm

Hot orange flames
roar northward
claim wooden shacks
rip through
everyday houses
elegant mansions
sacred gardens
the realm of Buddha

We scream against
harsh night winds
pray for rain
a Fireside chat
a pot of tea
traditions shatter
firewalls disappear
backfires cannot save us.

Weeks later
smoke gives way to
random destruction
a wet night
thundering nimbus clouds
We search for refuge
recover in one another
as through ashes we shift

Three Dogs

walking dogs, a Golden called Bella and Shepherd called Buddy,
twice daily the past few years.
approaching the neighbors and their Poodle called Teddy
begins the barking, snarling, threatening one another
passing by, dogs look over shoulders giving one more "just try it" growl
no reason whatsoever

acknowledgement of each other as we approach
making sure one set of us is on one side of the street
before the dogs begin their barrage of insults toward each other
then the fires came
the smoke was bad
no walking the dogs

five days past imminent threat, evacuations slowed,
though flames still raged over the hill,
my neighbors and I saw each other on our walk
this day we spoke
no move with courtesy across the street with shrugged shoulders
at the conflicting behavior from our dogs
approaching each other on the same side of the street
the three dogs just knew

we told of those who lost their homes, taking in evacuees
the good fortune of those left unscathed
keeping respectable distance
three dogs sat down
no pulling on leashes, no lunging toward the other,
only sitting down straight on haunches, but very polite
communities pulled together with kindness,
reaching for understanding, and allowing for grief and comfort
my neighbor and I were astonished,
even the dogs found neighborly compassion

Change of Plans

We haven't talked on the phone for this long in a while
I know, I was scheduled to work today and of all things to go to
    the Fire Fighter's Ball tonight
Obviously plans were changed
It was good to speak with you
I know, Mom, I love you

Elizabeth Klein

Silent Morning

I awoke to orange light,
beautiful really…
if it had smelled of oranges
rather than smoke.

As I made tea, washed my hair,
I asked myself…
who does these things
when the world is burning?
Who waters their plants
makes their bed?

When even the sparrows
sit in long silent rows
on wires waiting…

Henri Bensussen

Zone of Clearing

(Martha Lenio, HI-SEAS III commander:
"At the End of the Day You Don't Die.")

Fog today, no surround of vivid green
except the landscaped kind. I'm glassed
out, stuck inside with a worn gray
rug and a sprung chair, both flattened
as dead snakes in our dusty living room.
Coffee mug emptied, lamp clicked Off.

Home from a weekend immersed in pines
oaks, grasses, and wildflowers to study
a fire's aftermath of two decades back.
What happened, what now? Writing
a history to foretell a future. Where is
our Zone of Clearing to rein in destruction?

Hours from now other disasters may litter
this frayed carpet, yet somehow
we continue as if nothing has changed
like that fire's aftermath, nothing

and everything: topsoil dressed with ash
from incinerated trees, rare flowerings
making a comeback, seeds of pines
released to sprout and already tall. Birds
butterflies, bobcats, deer, all back along

with ticks and busy ants. Our aunts still
in their graves, we resigned to join them
but not today.

After

Standing like sentinels,
The remaining trees and vines shimmer and dance
Their golden, pumpkin, scarlet vestments shivering in the cool air
Sharp against the scorched and melted cocoa soil
Imbued with memories
Joy and toil
Vanished homes, vineyards, farms
Melted cars, discarded dreams
Echoing in silence
Rain soaking the earth with tears

Coming Through the Night

I didn't lose
    loved ones
      my home
not a single possession
to the fire

what I lost was something
    interior, a feeling of
    safety
that there will be no fireball

roaring down the mountain
    no frantic pounding on doors
    no fleeing through flames
    no nightgown on fire

that when I lay my head
on my pillow
give myself over to sleep
all I hold dear

will come through
    the night

Betty Les

Red, Orange and Yellow

I washed all the sheets
    cleaned my house
    swept the patios
    opened the mail
    paid the bills
    even read the enclosures

I baked cookies
    cooked dinner
    checked the bedroom door
one more time
finally crashed on the sofa
closed my eyes, exhausted.

Still, I see the map,
the fire
    where it is blazing
    where it has slowed
    what has been lost

etched on my eyelids
    in squares of
    red, orange and
    yellow

The Language of Fire

Not quite a hum nor whistle
the wind eerie
filling up space with madness.
Telephone warns.
Neighbor bangs at door.
Voices hysterical gathering pets.
The whoosh of movement
grabbing what only the mind
in seconds
thinks it must have.
And the wind
incessant,
playing its innocent, deadly
continuo and police car speakers
blaring
evacuate the area.

Car engine starts,
house deserted.
The piano, called grand
because of its splendor and
soaring authority
sighs as flames
lick at its legs.
Strings snap.
Wood crackles.
The great blackwing crashes,
soundboard collapses,
an inaudible groan.
This proud heirloom,
twists, buckles, melts,

soon to be unidentified
with the remaining rubble
and ashes,
not permitted to emote
one last dying
sweet note.

After the Fire

I distrust them now,
the red sunsets, the thick
hot wall of wind from
the east, the benign
smell of neighbor's chimneys—
all gone, not their chimneys but
so many others, vying with scorched
trees to be the last things up-
right in this new land-
scape, gray gaping where
the night's fire punched holes
into the city, insisted for once
we are not so different
from forests, we still
flee like all small
things do when the heat
curls the hair closest to
the skin, smoke will cure
you of softness, leave you
tough and dried of false
sentiment. After the fire
you will never forget.

Poet Biographies

Samantha C. Alban is a native Northern Californian. She is the author of contemporary fantasy and young adult fiction. She lives in Sonoma County with her family, three cats, and three lazy dogs. She loves hiking and music, and considers herself pretty darn lucky to live in such a beautiful place.

Barbara Armstrong, a lifelong disciple of poetry, enjoys exploring the nuanced power of words. A background in folk art and storytelling may be reflected in her poetry as she attempts to convey authentic images and sensations within a narrative. As a teacher, Barbara collaborated in the development of a language arts curriculum for use in elementary classrooms nationwide.

Judy M. Baker is a creative ambivert who broke the gender barrier in high school by enrolling in a boys-only class to print her poems and drawings. A voracious reader who attributes her love of books to her father. Her path in life is governed by communication: graphic design, marketing, coaching and writing.

Kitty (Catherine) Baker has long been focused on fiction writing for young audiences. Originally from Minnesota, she relocated to California in 2016. She has since joined Marin County Poet Laureate Prartho Sereno's Poetic Pilgrimage, exploring the power and playfulness of words and adding poetry to her writing repertoire.

Barbara Beatie is a local costumer and dresser at Transcendence Theatre where she was inspired and encouraged to revisit her writing. She became a writing student of Margaret Caminsky Shapiro in 2016 and joined Redwood Writers the same week. Poetry is her oldest love.

Dane Beatie is a senior at Santa Rosa High School. He enthusiastically thanks his literature teacher, Mrs. Kroeck, for inspiring a love of poetry and for the assignment that sparked this poem. Dane hopes to study history in college and to keep writing poetry.

Warren Bellows lives and writes his poetry in West County, Sonoma County. He is also a healer, author and visual artist. Warren has donated his painting "Hope" to Redwood Writers for the cover of *Phoenix*; he donated his work for the cover *Stolen Light*, the 2016 poetry anthology, too.

Jory Bellsey is an autodidact with a tendency to see the absurdity of it all. He is a very social being that prefers solitude more than company. He has interest and knowledge in an extensive array of domains. Jory is very new to poetry and this is his first publication.

Henri Bensussen has published poems in *Blue Mesa Review, Common Ground Review*, and *Sinister Wisdom*. Her poems have appeared in various anthologies. Finishing Line Press published her chapbook, *Earning Colors*, in 2015. She served on the board of the Mendocino Coast Writers Conference before moving to Santa Rosa in 2016.

Christine Berardo left a satisfying career writing TV movies and mini-series to work on a first novel. She's been writing poems, stories, song lyrics, and journals since childhood. Her poems and a short story have appeared in the Redwood Writers Anthologies *Stolen Light* and *Sonoma Stories*.

Lizette Black is the progeny of a pioneer ranching family from Sonoma County. As an introvert, she is most at home communing with nature. Poetry began to arise within her when words otherwise seemed to fail. She does not claim responsibility for poetic expressions, only for pruning them to look like poems.

Skye Blaine writes fiction, memoir, and poetry, developing themes of aging, coming of age, disability, and awakening. She received an MFA in Creative Writing from Antioch University. *Bound to Love: a memoir of grit and gratitude*, was published in 2015. Her debut novel, *Unleashed*, came out in November 2017.

Laura Blatt has worked as a laboratory technician, an editor/manager at a legal publishing company, and as a website writer. Her work has appeared in various journals, including *California Explorer, California Quarterly, Vintage Voices* and *Touch: A Journal of Healing.*

Jan Boddie, PhD, former psychotherapist and member of the first AIDS Unit Counseling Team, San Francisco General Hospital, has memoir stories published in seven anthologies. Though a few of her poems have been included in Redwood Writers "Poetry Place," this is Jan's first submission and acceptance in the Redwood Writers poetry anthology.

Catharine Bramkamp is a successful writing coach bringing her clients from idea to published book and beyond. She has written 17 novels and 3 books on writing. Her poetry appears in over a dozen anthologies including *And The Beats Go On* (she was editor as well) and the chapbook *Ammonia Sunrise* by Finishing Line Press.

Robbi Sommers Bryant's award-winning books include a novella, four novels, five short-story collections, and one book of poetry. Her work is published in magazines including *Readers Digest, Redbook, Penthouse,* college textbooks and several anthologies. Robbi's work has been optioned twice for TV's Movie of the Week. She is editor for the Redwood Writers anthology and serves as Vice President. She is a developmental, content and copy editor.

Simona Carini was born in Perugia, Italy. She is a graduate of the Catholic University of the Sacred Heart (Milan, Italy) and of Mills College (Oakland, CA). Simona Carini writes nonfiction and poetry and has been published in various venues, both in print and online. She lives in Northern California with her husband and works as an academic researcher in Medical Information Science.

Annita Clark-Weaver is the author of *Saudades: Brazilian Family Memories from Monarchy to Millennium*, a dual bicultural memoir spanning 150 years of Brazilian and US history, based on her Brazilian grandmother's posthumous journal and Annita's adventures in Brazil. Nowadays, she writes poetry inspired by her dreams, and stories for her grandchildren.

Ed Coletti is a poet, widely published internationally. He also is a painter and middling chess player. Most recent poetry collections were *Germs, Viruses & Catechisms* (2013 Civil Defense Press, SF) and *The Problem With Breathing* (Edwin Smith Publishing, Little Rock, 2015). Ed also curates the popular ten-year-old blog "No Money In Poetry." Coletti writes, "There was a time when I almost completely gave up writing. This was during the years 1973-1987. Then I reclaimed my soul and have written and published regularly again from 1987 to the present." Ed and Joyce Coletti lost their home in the 2017 fire.

Marlene Cullen feels deeply for the losses that too many experience. She believes that writing can lead to healing and free writes, inspired by writing prompts, can lead to transformational changes. Her poem in this anthology originated as a free write. She offers writing prompts on The Write Spot Blog.

Tina Riddle Deason has enjoyed writing since she was a young girl. She is currently working on her first novel *One's Own Sweet Way*. She is a Priestess and writes ritual and ceremony, as well as writing for her website. She resides in Sonoma County with her husband and family.

Rebecca del Rio resides in Northern California and Catalunya (Spain). She is a graduate of the University of Arizona Creative Writing Program, and has poetry published in literary journals in the United States, Canada, and Europe. Ms. del Rio's recently released book is *Prescription for the Disillusioned, Selected Poems* 2001–2016.

Geri Digiorno is founder and director of the Petaluma Poetry Walk going into its 22nd year. She was Poet Laureate of Sonoma County (2006-2007). Recent books are *White Lipstick* (Red Hen Press, 2005) and *Rosetta Mary* (dPress, 2007). Digiorno coordinated the Poetry & Music Series at the Redwood Cafe, Cotati. She is working on a new poetry book called *Bartali.*

Nancy Cavers Dougherty is the author of three chapbooks: *Tape Recorder On, Memory In Salt, Levee Town,* and *Silk,* a collaborative work. She advocates for several local organizations working on homelessness and child and family welfare issues. Nancy lives in Sebastopol, California with her husband, and family nearby. She is a cellist, collage artist and a grandma.

Terry Ehret has published four collections of poetry, most recently *Night Sky Journey.* She is a founding editor of Sixteen Rivers Press, and from 2004–2006 she served as poet laureate of Sonoma County where she lives and teaches writing workshops. In the summers, she offers travel programs for writers.

Adrienne Faulkner has lived in Santa Rosa for over forty years. She has only begun writing poetry in the last few years. Her poems often focus on her cats, dogs, wildlife and her garden. She writes also of experiences that have taught her about life. She often uses humor to paint pictures of the world around her.

Pamela Fender, author of *Beside Myself: Recovery From My Family Betrayal and Estrangement,* received her Bachelor of Arts degree in English at Sonoma State. She is a notary public and certified sign-ing agent. Raised in the suburbs of Los Angeles, she returned to Sonoma County after losing her home in the 1994 L.A. earthquake.

M. **Justine Foster** had an essay published in the *Big Brick Review*, Summer 2015 titled: "Firsts." A member of Redwood Writers Club, she has published poetry in the 2013 Anthology, *Water*, 2016 Anthology, *Stolen Light*, and their 2017 Anthology, *Sonoma—Stories of a Region and Its People*. She also has been a member of Wisconsin Writer's Association, and Wisconsin Fellowship of Poets since 2016.

Stephen Galiani holds an MFA in writing from the University of San Francisco and an MA in Humanities from Dominican University. Current occupations: writer, teacher, winery host, husband. Prior occupations: vagabond, social worker, investment manager, dad. His poetry and prose have been published by a number of small presses.

Rachel Garcia is a poet, musician and songwriter. She tours and performs full-time with her band *The Singer and The Songwriter*. She resides in the Bay Area with her partner, Thu, and her shih-tzu, Beatrice. She was most recently published in 2017 *Marin Poetry Center Anthology*.

Christina Gleason is a multimedia artist. She is often inspired by the informative language of nature. Christine finds passion and inspiration spending reflective moments on the the trails that bring shape and form to the art works that may come to be created.

Jeffrey "Jeff" Goldman is a native Californian. Born in Monterey. Raised in the Bay Area, a history graduate of Cal State Hayward, Jeff moved to Sonoma county from Sausalito in 1990. A true beginner in the writing community, this is his first foray into trying to be published.

Cristina Goulart's prose and poetry have appeared in Redwood Writers anthologies, and her articles addressing environmental issues have appeared in the *Windsor Times* and other community papers. Her story "Spare the Rod" was selected for the 2016 Lucky Penny Productions short story dramatic reading event in Napa, California.

John Hart of San Rafael is author of the poetry collections *The Climbers* (Pitt Poetry Series, 1978) and *Storm Camp* (Sugartown Publishing, 2017), as well as much nonfiction. He edits the venerable poetry triquarterly *Blue Unicorn* and works with poets in the Lawrence Hart Seminars, pursuing a tradition dating from the 1930s.

Katherine Hastings is the author of three collections of poetry, most recently *Shakespeare & Stein Walk Into a Bar* (Spuyten Duyvil NYC, 2016). Poet laureate emerita of Sonoma County, CA, Hastings founded the WordTemple Poetry Series and hosts WordTemple on KRCB FM. She is the editor of *Know Me Here—An Anthology of Poetry by Women* (WordTemple Press, 2017).

Karen Hayes grew up in Healdsburg, California, where she spent several formative years on the Russian River. She lives in Sonoma County, and loves spending time in Fort Bragg, California, where she gets most of her writing done. She currently has one book of poetry published, *River Stone*.

Pamela Heck is an artist, writer and special education teacher. She writes in a variety of genres including picture book, poetry, memoir and short story. Her entry in this year's club anthology was her first foray into nonfiction. Pamela is a recent addition to the Redwood Writers Board of Directors.

Lenore Hirsch has had a career in education as a teacher and administrator. She writes with humor about aging. She has written poetry, short stories, food and travel pieces. In 2013 she published *My Leash on Life, Foxy's View of the World from a Foot Off the Ground*.

Barbara Hirschfeld has been a writer all her life. She lives on eight acres in West Sebastopol and teaches meditation. She has a retreat center which she developed to provide people a peaceful place to work with their minds. She finds the process of writing poetry another valuable way to work with her mind.

Louise Hofmeister has had a career that included grant and report writing. Louise recently decided to pursue more creative forms of expression. Her poetry has been published in the anthology *Truth Serum*. Louise moved this summer to the Sonoma coast where she hangs out with birds, bats and the muse.

Iris Jamahl Dunkle is Poet Laureate of Sonoma County, CA. *Interrupted Geographies*, Trio House Press, is her third collection of poetry. Her previous collections are *There's a Ghost in this Machine of Air* (2015) and *Gold Passage* (2013). Iris Jamahl Dunkle teaches at Napa Valley College and is the Poetry Director of the Napa Valley Writers' Conference.

Natosi A.E. Johanna has been a writer, in one form or another, her entire life. Poetry was her first genre, but she has also penned fiction and creative nonfiction works. Natosi grew up in the pine forests of northern Minnesota, but has lived in California for the past forty years. Sonoma County has claimed her heart for the last twenty years.

Mara Lynn Johnstone grew up in a house on a hill, of which the top floor was built first. She lives in California with her husband, son, and laptop-loving cats. She enjoys writing, drawing, and spending hours discussing made-up things.

Briahn Kelly-brennan's sole purpose in writing is to make her feel, when she reads it, happy, content, satisfied, astounded, dreamy, or any kind of new and wonderful emotion. Because life can be hard, what one pays attention to grows, and why not focus on the half of glass that's full? She weaves into her writing her dedication to the earth, its animals, and its people.

James (Jim) Kelly is the former managing editor of *Laguna Life Magazine* and owner of High Plains Rider. He was also a reporter/columnist for newspapers and magazines from Vermont to California, including *The Sonoma Gazette*, *The Log*, *The Beacon* and the *La Jolla Light*.

Elizabeth Klein began writing poetry after she retired from running her own business for 35 years in San Francisco. What she loves most about poetry is how a simple thought, when looked at closely, opens up a whole world that before was unnoticed. Ideas for poems usually come when she's out walking. She lives in San Anselmo.

Christopher Layton was born in St. Louis in1938. He says creating beauty is in his blood. Both of his parents, his brother and his son are all architects. He grew up on the Mississippi River having a life filled with Tom Sawyer adventures. Positive experiences have given him his life's goal. He is committed to create positivity in a world where there can be so much that is negative.

Betty Les writes poetry and creative nonfiction, exploring the intersection of science and the mysteries of nature. Her poems have appeared in publications of the Redwood Writers and the Wisconsin Fellowship of Poets. A zoologist by training, she has also published widely on biodiversity.

Roger C. Lubeck is president of the Redwood Branch of the California Writers Club. He was the editor-in-chief on four anthologies including the *Redwood Writers 2016 Anthology: Untold Stories*. Roger's published works include seven novels, two business books, a produced ten-minute play, and a prize-winning short story.

Donald Mackay was born in San Francisco and has lived in Healdsburg with his wife and family for the past 20 years.

Ana Manwaring coaches and edits through JAM Manuscript Consulting and teaches creative writing through Napa Valley College. She has completed two thriller/suspense novels set in Mexico. Ana is active in CWC and Sisters in Crime.

Laura McHale Holland has published three award-winning books: the anthology *Sisters Born, Sisters Found: A Diversity of Voices on Sisterhood*; *The Ice Cream Vendor's Song*, a flash fiction collection; and *Reversible Skirt*, a childhood memoir. She has a new memoir *Resilient Ruin*.

Mark Meierding's poems have appeared in many local anthologies. He recently completed a Medieval fantasy novel, and one of his unique writings was a "sing-along oratorio for people who can't read music." Mark is a retired teacher and business systems analyst.

Phyllis Meshulam is the author of the full-length poetry book, *Land of My Father's War*, from Cherry Grove Collections, and other chapbooks. She teaches with California Poets in the Schools and coordinates "Poetry Out Loud." For CalPoets' 50th anniversary, She edited, *Poetry Crossing*, a joyful collection of lessons and poems.

Catherine Montague is a writer, professor, and researcher who divides her time between Sebastopol and Berkeley. Previous publications include poetry in the Redwood Writer's *Call of the Wild* anthology and the Point Reyes Seashore Association's newsletter.

Stephanie Moore is a recently retired English teacher from Santa Rosa. Her work has appeared in *The Sitting Room Anthology* and the *Marin Poetry Center Anthology*.

Clare Morris discovered poetry when she was the Founding Director of the Angela Center in Santa Rosa. She threaded poems through her workshops and retreats there, and began writing her own. She has published four collection of her poems, as well as a memoir.

Patricia Nelson is a retired attorney who has worked for many years with the Activist group of poets in Marin County. She has published two books, *Among the Shapes That Fold and Fly* and *Spokes of Dream or Bird*, recently published by Poetic Matrix Press. Two of her poems have been nominated for Pushcart Prizes.

Michael (Jack) O'Brien has published in print and on-line journals, most recently, *Blue Heron Review*, *Madness Muse Magazine*, *Ravens Perch*, and *Colloquial*. Also, his work has appeared in three anthologies: *Gridlock: Poetry of Southern California*, *Proposal on Brooklyn Bridge*, and *California: Dreams and Realities*.

Crystal Mazur Ockenfuss lives, reads, writes and teaches in the San Francisco Bay area. Her chapbook, "The Hobo Alphabet," appeared in 2013 with Dancing Girl Press of Chicago. She has recently had her poems published in *Ekphrasis, Slipstream, BelleSF* and *Datura.*

Gwynn O'Gara has published in *Paddlefish, Spoon River Poetry Review, Calyx, The Evansville Review,* and various anthologies. Her books include *Snake Woman Poems* and the chapbooks *Fixer-Upper, Winter at Green Haven,* and *Sea Cradles.* A long-time teacher with California Poets in the Schools, she served as Sonoma County Poet Laureate 2010 through 2011.

Jan Ogren, MFT is an international author, developmental editor, public speaker, shaman and licensed psychotherapist. She loves helping people rewrite their lives both through therapy and as an editor. *Choose Life: Poetry, Prose and Photography,* (2017) is in honor of her 98-year-old father's philosophy of life.

Renelaine Pfister's stories, essays and poems have been published in her native Philippines and in the U.S., including Vintage Voices 2012 and 2014, *And The Beats Go On,* YWCA's *Cry of the Nightbird, Filipino Fiction for Young Adults, Beyond Lumpia, Pansit and Seven Manangs Wild,* and *Healdsburg and Beyond.*

Ellie Portner is a poet and a visual artist. Her artwork can be seen at the Arts Guild of Sonoma gallery in the town of Sonoma. Ellie is a new member of Redwood Writers Club.

Carla Quint is a recent arrival to Marin County from San Francisco. She is a psychotherapist and her poems often draw from her work, but also from the abundant beauty of Marin County and her experience of urban life. Her free time is often spent along the Sonoma coast and traveling with her husband, Matt.

Jonah Raskin is the author of seven poetry chapbooks, including *The Fury of the Fires*. He performs his poetry with musicians, and he has just published his first murder mystery, "*Dark Land, Dark Mirror*," which is set in Sonoma County against a backdrop of extreme weather and global climate change.

Harry Reid is an architect, novelist, playwright who came to poetry writing for musical theater. The example here was written for Unis, a sightless young mole hiding in underground London during the War, telling the other creatures there how she perceives the coming of Spring.

Linda Loveland Reid is past president of Redwood Writers and a Jack London Award recipient. She has published two novels, is a figurative oil painter and theater director. Linda holds two *cum laude* degrees from SSU and currently teaches art history for SSU's Osher Lifelong Learning Institute.

Belinda Riehl's poetry is published in Medium.com and has won a haiku contest. Awarded the Redwood Writers 2015 Pullet Surprise, her volunteer work continued behind-the-scenes on Redwood Writers' 2016 *Untold Stories* as a proofreader, *2017 Sonoma* as a judge, story editor, and final reviewer, and *2018 Redemption* as Assistant Editor.

Jane Rinaldi is a former teacher working in several languages; it never occurred to her that she could throw her accumulated knowledge into one big washing machine to see what unexpected rhythms and rhymes would result. She is now retired, living in Santa Rosa and enjoying the inspiration of nature up close.

Larry Robinson is a potter, a retired psychotherapist and a recovering politician. His calling is to restore the soul of the world through reviving the oral tradition of poetry. He is the founder and producer of Rumi's Caravan and serves on the boards of directors for the Center for Climate Protection and Meridian University.

Elaine Rock has enjoyed writing poetry since high school. This is her first poetry submission for publication. She writes biography, historical fiction and short stories about exceptional and inspiring women who have been neglected or forgotten by history. Elaine is currently a vice-president of the Redwood Writers Club.

Lilith Rogers loves living in and is inspired daily by beautiful Northern California. Here she writes her poetry, memoir, plays, children's stories, and more. And she knows it will take time but we will recover from these fire storms. Lilith also performs "Rachel Carson Returns."

Margaret Rooney is a retired psychotherapist who enjoys making jewelry and writing poetry. She finds the process of forming, framing and pinning a poem fascinating and exhilarating, like flying on a trapeze, whizzing through the air, flung high and wide over the world; hanging on the breathtaking possibility of either making a startling connection or falling to the net and bouncing for a bit.

Luis Salvago-Toledo was born and raised in Málaga (Spain), where he attended the Merchant Marine Academy, Master. After sailing as a deck officer for over 10 years, he settled down in California. Here he worked in the computer field while studying philosophy (BA UCLA, MA UC Berkeley). Today a retiree, he enjoys tutoring Spanish and occasionally writing newspaper columns.

Maryann Schacht wrote an advice column in Albany NY, was a staff writer at OF Westchester. Her book *A Caregivers Challenge* was a semi-finalist for IBPA Book Award 1995. *Pan: the Trickster* was published in 2013. Writing has been the underpinning theme of Maryann Schacht's life.

Alicia Schooler-Hugg is a former op-ed columnist and features writer for *The (Stockton) Record, Modesto Bee, Nurseweek*, and *nurse.com*. As a registered nurse, she taught university level communications courses and received several journalism-based awards. She has authored two books: *Art and Soul of Jazz, A Tribute to Charles Mingus, Jr.* and *Granny Does Europe: A Love Story.*

Florentia Scott lived in Canada for many years, working as a corporate communicator and journalist before retiring in Santa Rosa. She writes novels and is gathering her poems into a chapbook. Her work has appeared in *Ascent Aspirations* magazine, the *Alberni Valley Times*, and the San Francisco Writers Conference Anthology.

Jan Seagrave earned a living through words and books, and now retired, is writing poetry again. Her work has recently appeared in the 2016 and 2017 Marin Poetry Anthologies and in *Amore: Love Poems,* ed. J. Tucker. She tries to take things literally when necessary.

Joanell Serra MFT lives and writes in Northern California. An award winning writer, she is a playwright, novelist, nonfiction and short story writer. Her first novel, *The Vines We Planted,* will be out in May 2018 with Wido publishing.

Robert Shafer, a member of Redwood Writers, grew up as a Chicago slum boy and an abandoned child. Those early years inspire much of his writing. He served four years in the US Navy and worked thirty-five-years as a film/video editor in San Francisco. He currently resides in Napa, California.

Jo Ann Smith spent most of her life in public education as a teacher, counselor, vice principal, principal, assistant superintendent and for the last twelve years of her career as superintendent, all at the high school level. Now retired, she finds herself drawn to the evocative nature of poetry, a challenging, revealing, and liberating journey. Jo Ann lives happily in Sebastopol with her partner, Gale, and their Standard Poodle, Gracie.

Linda Stamps established careers in community organizing, professional football, law, journalism and higher education. She worked on staff at the *Mendocino Beacon* and the *Fort Bragg Advocate News* covering sports and features. She has published articles in *Out in All Directions,* an LGBTQ history and almanac. Linda is a new poet.

Deborah Taylor-French writes mystery and poetry. She blogs to save dogs' lives and dog lovers' sanity at the website Dog Leader Mysteries. As Redwood Writers' Author Support Facilitator, Deborah volunteers as a writer helping writers. She writes the column, "Cotati Heart & Soul" for the monthly *Sonoma County Gazette.*

Nina Tepedino has been writing poetry since 1975. She is part of the rich West Sonoma County literary culture, where many poets thrive and create. She lives in the community of Sebastopol, California.

Bill Vartnaw, Sonoma County Poet Laureate Emeritus, was born and raised in Petaluma. He's publisher of Taurean Horn Press, an independent poetry press started in San Francisco in 1974, and author of two books of poetry, *In Concern: for Angels* (THP, 1984); *Suburbs of my Childhood* (Beatitude Press, 2009) & 3 chapbooks.

Annita Clark-Weaver is the author of *Saudades: Brazilian Family Memories from Monarchy to Millennium,* a dual memoir spanning 150 years of Brazilian and US history. She loves to swim, dance, laugh, and make art with her three grandchildren, and enjoys family celebrations and sharing life's joys and sorrows with friends.

Arte L. Whyte lives in Northern California. He has written and published poetry and re-writes for Universal Studios. His derivative of Harry Nilsson's "Land of Point" is at the Library of Congress. He has published one sci-fi novel *The Children of the Stars.* He is currently working on book two.

Jim Wilder has been writing poetry and music in Spanish as a way to learn the language. He has had one of his songs sung at the Rosquilla Festival in Somoto, Nicaragua. Besides writing, Jim is working with a non-profit in Nicaragua to create and promote music delegations

Nathaniel Robert "Bob" Winters grew up in suburban NYC. Upon completing a tour in the Navy, he fell in love with and settled in Northern California. Bob earned a BA from Sonoma State University and a Master's from CSU Stanislaus. The retired teacher lives with his wife/muse in the Napa Valley. Despite having Parkinson's disease, he writes almost every day and has published fifteen books in the last ten years.

Marilyn Wolters has lived in Sonoma County for over thirty-five years. She spent most of her working years helping disabled college students develop essay-writing skills. Now retired, she can't resist writing regularly. Her short pieces have been published and performed.

Jean Wong, author of *Sleeping with the Gods* and *Hurtling Jade*, is an award winning poet, fiction, and memoir writer. Her work has been produced by the 6th Street Playhouse and other theater venues. Jean writes from the bottom of a well, always amazed to look up and see the sky.

The Editorial Staff

Les Bernstein's poems have appeared in journals, presses and anthologies internationally and in the U.S. Her chapbooks *Borderland, Naked Little Creatures* and *Amid the Din* have been published by Finishing Line Press. Les is a winner of the 6th annual Nazim Hikmet Festival. She is a 2015 Pushcart Prize nominee. She is the Marin High School Poetry Contest and Anthology coordinator and judge. Les lives in Mill Valley with her enormous family.

Fran Claggett-Holland teaches poetry and memoir writing through OLLI and in her home. She edited *Stolen Light*, the 2016 Redwood Writers poetry anthology and is co-editor with Les Bernstein of *Phoenix*. Bill Vartnaw's Taurean Horn Press published her first poetry collection, *Black Birds and Other Birds* while Charlie Pendergast's RiskPress published her second, *Crow Crossings*. Last summer she launched her latest book, *Moments with Madge: Lux Aeterna*, which features a cover painting by Linda Reid, interior paintings by Warren Bellows and nature photography by Ron Brown. *Moments* is a poetic tribute in honor and memory of her life partner Madge Holland.

Judy Anderson is a California native, these days meandering between Marin and the Trinity wilderness. The river and surrounding landscape inspire a transcendent poetry of place. Her life work as a graphic designer has left its mark in the visual imagery of her poetry. Her poems have appeared in more than a dozen anthologies.

Susan Gunter is a Professor of English Emerita. In addition to publishing three books on the James Family, she has published poems in journals around the country, including *Atlanta Review* and *Louisville Review*. She won a fifth place award in last year's *Writer's Digest* national poetry contest.

Redwood Branch History

Jack London was first attracted to the beauty of Sonoma County in 1909, the very year he was named an honorary founding member of the Berkeley-based California Writers Club [CWC].

In 1975 Redwood Writers was established as the fourth CWC branch, due to special impetus from Helene S. Barnhart of the Berkeley Branch, who had relocated to the North Bay. She and forty-five charter members founded the Redwood Branch of the CWC.

Redwood Writers is a non-profit organization whose motto is: "writers helping writers." Their mission is to provide a friendly, inclusive and inspirational environment in which members may meet, network, and learn about the writing industry.

Monthly meetings are open to the public and feature professional speakers who present a variety of topics, from writing skills to publishing and marketing.

The club sponsors a variety of activities such as Contest and Workshops. Every other year the club holds a Writers Conference, a day-long event offering seminars on all areas of writing, taught by professionals from various areas of the state.

Redwood Writers publishes a members' anthology, now celebrating thirteen consecutive years. This is in addition to a Poetry Anthology that is published every other year.

In cooperation with the county's largest bookstore, Copperfield's Books, Redwood Writers presents "Hot Summer Nights," where members' books are reviewed for discussion at meetings open to the general public.

An extensive monthly newsletter and award winning website, along with other social media outlets, keeps members in touch and gives them the chance to share accomplishments and successes.

Redwood Writers is indebted to its founders and charter members, to the leaders who have served at the helm, and to our many members. Without this volunteer dedication, Redwood Writers could not have developed into the professional club it is today with over 350 members. For more information visit *www.redwoodwriters.org*.

Redwood Writers Presidents

1975	Helen Schellenberg Barnhart	1992	Barb Truax (4 years)
1976	Dianne Kurlfinke	1997	Marvin Steinbock (2 years)
1977	Natlee Kenoyer	1999	Dorothy Molyneaux
1978	Inman Whipple	2000	Carol McConkie
1979	Herschel Cozine	2001	Gil Mansergh (2 years)
1980	Edward Dolan	2003	Carol McConkie
1981	Alla Crone Hayden	2004	Charles Brashear
1982	Mildred Fish	2005	Linda C. McCabe (2 years)
1983	Waldo Boyd	2007	Karen Batchelor (2 years)
1984	Margaret Scariano	2009	Linda Loveland Reid (3 years)
1985	Dave Arnold	2013	Robbi Sommers Bryant (1.5 years)
1986	Mary Priest (2 years)	2015	Sandy Baker (2 years)
1988	Marion McMurtry (2 years)	2017	Roger C. Lubeck
1990	Mary Varley (2 years)		

Awards

Jack London Award

Every other year, CWC branches may nominate a member to receive the Jack London Award for outstanding service to the branch, sponsored by CWC Central. The recipients are:

1975	Helen Schellenberg Barnhart	1998	Barbara Truax
1977	Dianne Kurlfinke	2003	Nadenia Newkirk
1979	Peggy Ray	2004	Gil Mansergh
1981	Pat Patterson	2005	Mary Rosenthal
1983	Inman Whipple	2007	Catherine Keegan
1985	Ruth Irma Walker	2009	Karen Batchelor
1987	Margaret Scariano	2011	Linda C. McCabe
1989	Mary Priest	2013	Linda Loveland Reid
1991	Waldo Boyd	2015	Jeane Slone
1993	Alla Crone Hayden	2017	Sandy Baker
1995	Mildred Fish		
1997	Mary Varley		

Helene S. Barnhart Award

In 2010 this award was instituted, inspired by Redwood Writers first president, to honor outstanding service to the branch, given in alternating years of the Jack London Award.

2010	Kate (Catharine) Farrell	2016	Robin Moore
2012	Ana Manwaring	2018	Malena Eljumaily
2014	Juanita J. Martin		

Additional copies
of this book
may be purchased at
amazon.com
and other retail outlets.

www.ingramcontent.com/pod-product-compliance
Lightning Source LLC
Chambersburg PA
CBHW051815090426

42736CB00011B/1495